W0246884

PENGUIN BOOKS

THE BOOK OF NATURE

Ruskin Bond's first novel, *The Room on the Roof*, written when he was seventeen, received the John Llewellyn Rhys Memorial Prize in 1957. Since then he has written a number of novellas, essays, poems and children's books, many of which have been published by Penguin. He has also written over 500 short stories and articles that have appeared in magazines and anthologies. He received the Sahitya Akademi Award in 1993, the Padma Shri in 1999 and the Padma Bhushan in 2014.

Ruskin Bond was born in Kasauli, Himachal Pradesh, and grew up in Jamnagar, Dehradun, New Delhi and Shimla. As a young man, he spent four years in the Channel Islands and London. He returned to India in 1955. He now lives in Landour, Mussoorie, with his adopted family.

THE
BOOK OF
NATURE

RUSKIN
BOND

PENGUIN BOOKS

An imprint of Penguin Random House

PENGUIN BOOKS

USA | Canada | UK | Ireland | Australia
New Zealand | India | South Africa | China | Singapore

Penguin Books is part of the Penguin Random House group of companies
whose addresses can be found at global.penguinrandomhouse.com

Published by Penguin Random House India Pvt. Ltd
4th Floor, Capital Tower 1, MG Road,
Gurugram 122 002, Haryana, India

First published in Viking by Penguin Books India 2004
Published in Penguin Books 2008
This edition published in Penguin Books 2016

10 9 8 7 6 5 4 3 2

ISBN 9780143426684

Typeset in Sabon Roman by SÜRYA, New Delhi
Printed at Manipal Technologies Limited, India

Contents

The nightmare of modern cheapjack life was all explained . . . [a] symptom of deep disorder; all due, this feverish external business, to an odd misunderstanding with the Earth. Humanity had somehow quarrelled with her, claiming an independence that could not really last. For her the centuries of this estrangement was but a little thing perhaps—a moment or two in that huge life which counted a million years to lay a narrow bed of chalk. They would come back in time. Meanwhile she ever called. A few, perhaps, already dreamed of return . . . They heard, these few, the splendid whisper that, sweetly calling, ever passed about the world.'

—Algernon Blackwood,
The Centaur *(1911)*

Introduction

My introduction to the world of Nature was a painful one. Aged five, I was coming down the spiral staircase from the roof of our bungalow in Jamnagar State, when inadvertently I dislodged a beehive under one of the steps. I was immediately attacked by a swarm of angry bees, who proceeded to sting me on my face, arms and legs. I got down the stairs and ran indoors, screaming for help.

Help came in the form of my father, who calmed me down and bathed me in a solution of potassium permanganate. After two feverish days in bed, I was up and about again. But I'd learnt that Nature isn't always birdsong and dew-drenched daffodils.

There were other, more pleasant, aspects of the natural world that remain in my memory: collecting seashells on the beach, feeding the turkeys on the State's turkey farm, wandering through a glade of tall cosmos flowers, watching the village boys wash down their buffaloes at the edge of the lake.

I grew up with an awareness of my natural surroundings—bee stings and all—and later this was buttressed by the sort of books and stories that I enjoyed reading—*Peter Pan in Kensington Gardens*, the wonderland of Alice, the Mowgli stories, Ballantyne's *Coral Island* and *Hudson Bay*, Jack London's *White Fang*, the *Panchatantra* and *Jataka Tales* . . .

The literature that came my way between the ages of five and fifteen was of a kind that is rare today, for most modern writers appear to be preoccupied with urban backgrounds and concerns. I wish there was a Thoreau around, or a Richard Jefferies, or an H.E. Bates: writers who lived close to Nature and made it a part of their creative work.

I have done my best to follow in their footsteps—observing and recording the natural life around me, and working it into my stories, essays and poems. A comprehensive selection of these 'Nature writings' (spanning half a century!) is presented here. This is not a book of natural history, rather a record of my relationship with the natural world, which has sustained and inspired me over the years.

This is a relationship that has grown stronger and more meaningful ever since I came to live in the hills over forty years ago. 'Is Nature your religion?' someone asked, just the other day. It would be presumptuous to say so. Nature doesn't promise you anything—an after life, rewards for good behaviour, protection from enemies, wealth, happiness, progeny, all the things that humans desire and pray for. No,

Nature does not promise these things. Nature is a reward in itself.

It is there, to be appreciated, to be understood, to be lived and loved. And in its way it gives us everything—the bounty and goodness of the earth, the sea, the sky. Food, water, the air we breathe. All the things we take for granted.

And sometimes, when we take it too much for granted, or misuse its generosity, it turns against us and unleashes forces that overwhelm us—earthquake, tidal wave, typhoon, flood, drought. But then, Nature settles down again and resumes its generous ways. For it is all about renewal—seasons and the weather, sunlight and darkness, the urgency of growth, the fertility of the seed and the egg. Governments rise and fall, machines rust away, great buildings crumble, but mountains still stand, rivers flow to the sea, and the earth is clothed with grass and verdure.

Nature gives. And takes away. And *gives again*.

RUSKIN BOND
August 2004

I
Grandfather's Zoo

Back in the 1930s and '40s, when Dehra was just a small town, most of the bungalows had large compounds—gardens in front, orchards at the back, and sometimes a bit of wilderness thrown in.

Growing up in these surroundings, one was bound to come into close contact with the natural world—the denizens of the banyan and jackfruit trees: birds, butterflies, squirrels, reptiles. And then there were the unusual pets that Grandfather brought home from time to time . . .

Though the house and grounds of our home in Dehra were Grandfather's domain—where he kept an odd assortment of pets—the magnificent old banyan tree was mine, chiefly because Grandfather, at the age of sixty-five, could no longer climb it. Grandmother used to tease him about this, and would speak of a certain Countess of Desmond, an Englishwoman who lived to the age of hundred and seventeen, and would have lived longer if she hadn't fallen while climbing an apple tree. The spreading branches of the banyan tree, which curved to the ground and took root again, forming a maze of arches, gave me endless pleasure. The tree was older than the house, older than Grandfather, as old as the town of Dehra, nestling in a valley at the foot of the Himalayas.

My first friend and familiar was a small grey squirrel. Arching his back and sniffing into the air, he seemed at first to resent my invasion of his privacy. But when he found that I did not arm myself with a catapult or air-gun, he became friendlier. And when I started leaving him pieces of cake and biscuit, he grew bolder, and finally became familiar enough to take food from my hands.

Before long he was delving into my pockets and helping himself to whatever he could find. He was a very young squirrel, and his friends and relatives probably thought him headstrong and foolish for trusting a human.

In the spring, when the banyan tree was full of small red figs, birds of all kinds would flock into its branches, the red-bottomed bulbul, cheerful and greedy; gossiping rosy-pastors; and parrots and crows, squabbling with each other all the time. During the fig season, the banyan tree was the noisiest place on the road.

Halfway up the tree I had built a small platform on which I would often spend the afternoons when it wasn't too hot. I could read there, propping myself up against the bole of the tree with the cushions taken from the drawing room. *Treasure Island*, Huck Finn, the Mowgli Stories, and detective novels made up my bag of very mixed reading.

When I didn't want to read, I could look down through the banyan leaves at the world below, at Grandmother hanging up or taking down the washing, at the cook quarrelling with a fruit vendor, or at Grandfather grumbling at the hardy Indian marigold, which insisted on springing up all over his very English garden. Usually nothing very exciting happened while I was in the banyan tree, but on one particular afternoon I had enough excitement to last me through the summer.

That was the time I saw a mongoose and a cobra fight to death in the garden, while I sat directly above them in the banyan tree.

It was an April afternoon. The warm breezes of approaching summer had sent everyone, including Grandfather, indoors. I was feeling drowsy myself and was wondering if I should go to the pond behind the house for a swim, when I saw a huge black cobra gliding out of a clump of cacti and making for some cooler part of the garden. At the same time a mongoose (whom I had often seen) emerged from the bushes and went straight for the cobra.

In a clearing beneath the tree, in bright sunshine, they came face to face.

The cobra knew only too well that the grey mongoose, three feet long, was a superb fighter, clever and aggressive. But the cobra was a skilful and experienced fighter too. He could move swiftly and strike with the speed of light, and the sacs behind his long, sharp fangs were full of deadly venom.

It was to be a battle of champions.

Hissing defiance, his forked tongue darting in and out, the cobra raised three of his six feet off the ground, and spread his broad, spectacled hood. The mongoose bushed his tail. The long hair on his spine stood up (in the past, the very thickness of his hair had saved him from bites that would have been fatal to others).

Though the combatants were unaware of my presence in the banyan tree, they soon became aware of the arrival of two other spectators. One was a myna, and the other a jungle crow (not the wily urban crow). They had seen these preparations for battle, and had settled on the cactus to watch the outcome. Had they been content only to watch, all would have been well with both of them.

The cobra stood on the defensive, swaying slowly from side to side, trying to mesmerize the mongoose into making a false move. The mongoose knew the power of his opponent's glassy, twinkling eyes, and refused to meet them. Instead, he fixed his gaze at a point just below the cobra's hood, and opened the attack.

Moving forward quickly until he was just within the cobra's reach, he made a feint to one side. Immediately the cobra struck. His great hood came down so swiftly that I thought nothing could save the mongoose. But the little fellow jumped neatly to one side, and darted in as swiftly as the cobra, biting the snake on the back and darting away again out of reach.

The moment the cobra struck, the crow and the myna hurled themselves at him, only to collide heavily in mid-air. Shrieking at each other, they returned to the cactus plant.

A few drops of blood glistened on the cobra's back.

The cobra struck again and missed. Again the mongoose sprang aside, jumped in and bit. Again the birds dived at the snake, bumped into each other instead, and returned shrieking to the safety of the cactus.

The third round followed the same course as the first but with one dramatic difference. The crow and the myna, still determined to take part in the proceedings, dived at the cobra, but this time they missed each other as well as their mark. The myna flew on and reached its perch, but the crow tried to pull up in mid-air and turn back. In the second that it took him to do this, the cobra whipped his head back and struck with great force, his snout thudding against the crow's body.

I saw the bird flung nearly twenty feet across the garden, where, after fluttering about for a while, it lay still. The myna remained on the cactus plant, and when the snake and the mongoose returned to the fray, it very wisely refrained from interfering again!

The cobra was weakening, and the mongoose, walking fearlessly up to it, raised himself on his short legs, and with a lightning snap had the big snake by the snout. The cobra writhed and lashed about in a frightening manner, and even coiled itself about the mongoose, but all to no avail. The little fellow hung grimly on, until the snake had ceased to struggle. He then smeared along its quivering length, gripping it round the hood, and dragging it into the bushes.

The myna dropped cautiously to the ground, hopped about, peered into the bushes from a safe distance, and then, with a shrill cry of congratulation, flew away.

When I had also made a cautious descent from the tree and returned to the house, I told Grandfather of the fight I had seen. He was pleased that the mongoose had won. He had encouraged it to live in the garden, to keep away the snakes, and fed it regularly with scraps from the kitchen. He had never tried taming it, because a wild mongoose was more useful than a domesticated one.

From the banyan tree I often saw the mongoose patrolling the four corners of the garden, and once I saw him with an egg in his mouth and knew he had been in the poultry house; but he hadn't harmed the birds, and I knew Grandmother would forgive him for stealing as long as he kept the snakes away.

The banyan tree was also the setting for what we were to call the Strange Case of the Grey Squirrel and the White Rat.

The white rat was Grandfather's—he had bought it from the bazaar for four annas—but I would often take it with me into the banyan tree, where it soon struck up a friendship with one of the squirrels. They would go off together on little excursions among the roots and branches of the old tree.

Then the squirrel started building a nest. At first she tried building it in my pockets, and when I went indoors and changed my clothes I would find straw and grass falling out. Then one day Grandmother's knitting was missing. We hunted for it everywhere but without success.

Next day I saw something glinting in the hole in the banyan tree and, going up to investigate, saw that it was the end of Grandmother's steel knitting-needle. On looking further, I discovered that the hole was crammed with knitting. And amongst the wool were three baby squirrels—all of them white!

Grandfather had never seen white squirrels before, and we gazed at them in wonder. We were puzzled for some time, but when I mentioned the white rat's frequent visits to the tree, Grandfather told me that the rat must be the father. Rats and squirrels were related to each other, he said, and so it was quite possible for them to have offspring—in this case, white squirrels!

The Elephant and the Cassowary Bird

The baby elephant, another of Grandfather's unusual pets, wasn't out of place in our home in north India because India is where elephants belong, and in any case our house was full of pets brought home by Grandfather, who was in the Forest Service. But the cassowary bird was different. No one had ever seen such a bird before—not in India, that is. Grandfather had picked it up on a voyage to Singapore, where he'd been given the bird by a rubber planter who'd got it from a Dutch trader who'd got it from a man in Indonesia.

Anyway, it ended up at our home in Dehra, and seemed to do quite well in the sub-tropical climate. It looked like a cross between a turkey and an ostrich, but bigger than the former and smaller than the latter—about five feet in height. It was not a beautiful bird, nor even a friendly one, but it had come to stay, and everyone was curious about it, especially the baby elephant.

Right from the start the baby elephant took a great interest in the cassowary. He would circle round the odd creature, and diffidently examine with his trunk the texture of its stumpy wings; of course, he suspected no evil, and his childlike curiosity encouraged him to take liberties which resulted in an unpleasant experience.

Noticing the baby elephant's attempts to make

friends with the rather morose cassowary, we felt a bit apprehensive. Self-contained and sullen, the big bird responded only by slowly and slyly raising one of its powerful legs, all the while gazing into space with an innocent air. We knew what the gesture meant: we had seen that treacherous leg raised on many an occasion, and suddenly shooting out with a force that would have done credit to a vicious camel. In fact, camel and cassowary kicks are delivered on the same plan, except that the camel kicks backward like a horse and the bird forward.

We wished to spare our baby elephant a painful experience, and led him away from the bird. But he persisted in his friendly overtures, and one morning he received an ugly reward. Rapid as lightning, the cassowary hit straight from the hip and knee joints, and the elephant ran squealing to Grandfather.

For several days he avoided the cassowary, and we thought he had learnt his lesson. He crossed and recrossed the compound and the garden, swinging his trunk, thinking furiously. Then, a week later, he appeared on the veranda at breakfast time in his usual cheery, childlike fashion, sidling up to the cassowary as if nothing had happened.

We were struck with amazement at this and so, it seemed, was the bird. Had the painful lesson already been forgotten, that too by a member of the elephant tribe noted for its ability never to forget? Another dose of the same medicine would serve the booby right.

The cassowary once more began to draw up its fighting leg with sinister determination. It was nearing the true position for the master-kick, kung-fu style, when all of a sudden the baby elephant seized with his trunk the other leg of the cassowary and pulled it down. There was a clumsy flapping of wings, a tremendous swelling of the bird's wattle, and an undignified getting up, as if it were a floored boxer doing his best to beat the count of ten. The bird then marched off with an attempt to look stately and unconcerned, while we at the breakfast table were convulsed with laughter.

After this the cassowary bird gave the baby elephant as wide a berth as possible. But they were forced not to co-exist for very long. The baby elephant, getting bulky and cumbersome, was sold to a zoo where he became a favourite with young visitors who loved to take rides on his back.

As for the cassowary, he continued to grace our veranda for many years, gaped at but not made much of, while entering on a rather friendless old age.

Owls In the Family

One winter morning, my grandfather and I found a baby spotted owlet by the veranda steps of our home in Dehradun. When Grandfather picked it up the owlet hissed and clacked its bill but then, after a meal of raw meat and water, settled down under my bed.

Spotted owlets are small birds. A fully grown one is no larger than a thrush and they have none of the sinister appearance of large owls. I had once found a pair of them in our mango tree and by tapping on the tree trunk had persuaded one to show an enquiring face at the entrance to its hole. The owlet is not normally afraid of man nor is it strictly a night bird. But it prefers to stay at home during the day as it is sometimes attacked by other birds who consider all owls their enemies.

The little owlet was quite happy under my bed. The following day we found a second baby owlet in almost the same spot on the veranda and only then did we realize that where the rainwater pipe emerged through the roof, there was a rough sort of nest from which the birds had fallen. We took the second young owl to join the first and fed them both.

When I went to bed, they were on the window ledge just inside the mosquito netting and later in the night, their mother found them there. From outside, she crooned and gurgled for a long time and in the morning, I found she had left a mouse with its tail tucked through the netting. Obviously, she put no great trust in me as a foster parent.

The young birds thrived and ten days later, Grandfather and I took them into the garden to release them. I had placed one on a branch of the mango tree and was stooping to pick up the other when I received a heavy blow on the back of the head. A second or two later, the mother owl swooped down on Grandfather but he was quite agile and ducked out of the way.

Quickly, I placed the second owl under the mango tree. Then from a safe distance we watched the mother fly down and lead her offspring into the long grass at the edge of the garden. We thought she would take her family away from our rather strange household but next morning I found the two owlets perched on the hatstand in the veranda.

I ran to tell Grandfather and when we came back we found the mother sitting on the birdbath a few metres away. She was evidently feeling sorry for her behaviour the previous day because she greeted us with a soft 'whoo-whoo'.

'Now there's an unselfish mother for you,' said Grandfather. 'It's obvious she wants us to keep an eye on them. They're probably getting too big for her to manage.'

So the owlets became regular members of our household and were among the few pets that Grandmother took a liking to. She objected to all snakes, most monkeys and some crows—we'd had all these pets from time to time—but she took quite a fancy to the owlets and frequently fed them spaghetti!

They loved to sit and splash in a shallow dish provided by Grandmother. They enjoyed it even more if cold water was poured over them from a jug while they were in the bath. They would get thoroughly wet, jump out and perch on a towel rack, shake themselves and return for a second splash and sometimes a third. During the day they dozed on a hatstand. After dark, they had the freedom of the house and their nightly occupation was catching beetles, the kitchen quarters being a happy hunting ground. With their razor-sharp eyes and powerful beaks, they were excellent pest-destroyers.

Looking back on those childhood days, I carry in my mind a picture of Grandmother in her rocking chair with a contented owlet sprawled across her aproned lap. Once, on entering a room while she was taking an afternoon nap, I saw one of the owlets had crawled up her pillow till its head was snuggled under her ear.

Both Grandmother and the owlet were snoring.

Travelling with Grandfather's Zoo

'All aboard!' shrieked Popeye, Grandmother's pet parrot, as the family climbed aboard the Lucknow

Express. We were moving for some months from Dehra to Lucknow, and as Grandmother had insisted on taking her parrot along, Grandfather and I insisted on bringing our pets too—a teenaged tiger (Grandfather's) and a small squirrel (mine). But we thought it prudent to leave the python behind.

In those days trains in India were not so crowded and it was possible to travel with a variety of creatures. Grandfather had decided to do things in style by travelling first-class, so we had a four-berth compartment of our own, and Timothy, the tiger, had an entire berth to himself. Later, everyone agreed that Timothy behaved perfectly throughout the journey. Even the guard admitted that he could not have asked for a better passenger: no stealing from vendors, no shouting at coolies, no breaking of railway property, no spitting on the platform.

All the same, the journey was not without incident and before we reached Lucknow, there was excitement enough for everyone.

To begin with, Popeye objected to vendors and other people poking their hands in through the windows. Before the train had moved out of the Dehra station, he had nipped two fingers and tweaked a ticket inspector's ear.

No sooner had the train started moving than Chips, my squirrel, emerged from my pocket to examine his surroundings. Before I could stop him, he was out of the compartment door, scurrying along the corridor.

Chips discovered that the train was a squirrel's paradise, almost all the passengers having bought large quantities of roasted peanuts before the train pulled out. He had no difficulty in making friends with both children and grown-ups, and it was an hour before he returned to our compartment, his tummy almost bursting.

'I think I'll go to sleep,' said Grandmother, covering herself with a blanket and stretching out on the berth opposite Timothy's. 'It's been a tiring day.'

'Aren't you going to eat anything?' asked Grandfather.

'I'm not hungry—I had some soup before we left. You two help yourselves from the tiffin basket.'

Grandmother dozed off, and even Popeye started nodding, lulled to sleep by the clackety-clack of the wheels and the steady puffing of the steam engine.

'Well, I'm hungry,' I said. 'What did Granny make for us?'

'Ham sandwiches, boiled eggs, a roast chicken, gooseberry pie. It's all in the tiffin basket under your berth.'

I tugged at the large basket and dragged it into the centre of the compartment. The straps were loosely tied. No sooner had I undone them than the lid flew open, and I let out a gasp of surprise.

In the basket was Grandfather's pet python, curled up contentedly on the remains of our dinner.

Grandmother had insisted that we leave the python behind, and Grandfather had let it loose in the garden. Somehow, it had managed to snuggle itself into the tiffin basket.

'Well, what are you staring at?' asked Grandfather from his corner.

'It's the python,' I said. 'And it has finished all our dinner.'

Grandfather joined me, and together we looked down at what remained of the food. Pythons don't chew, they swallow: outlined along the length of the large snake's sleek body were the distinctive shapes of a chicken, a pie, and six boiled eggs. We couldn't make out the ham sandwiches, but presumably these had been eaten too because there was no sign of them in the basket. Only a few apples remained. Evidently, the python did not care for apples.

Grandfather snapped the basket shut and pushed it back beneath the berth.

'We mustn't let Grandmother see him,' he said. 'She might think we brought him along on purpose.'

'Well, I'm hungry,' I complained. Just then, Chips returned from one of his forays and presented me with a peanut.

'Thanks,' I said. 'If you keep bringing me peanuts all night, I might last until morning.'

But it was not long before I felt sleepy. Grandfather had begun to nod and the only one who was wide awake was the squirrel, still intent on investigating distant compartments.

A little after midnight there was a great clamour at the end of the corridor. Grandfather and I woke up. Timothy growled in his sleep, and Popeye made complaining noises.

Suddenly there were cries of 'Saap, saap!' (Snake, snake!)

Grandfather was on his feet in a moment. He looked under the berth. The tiffin basket was empty.

'The python's out,' he said, and dashed out of our compartment in his pyjamas. I was close behind.

About a dozen passengers were bunched together outside the washroom door.

'Anything wrong?' asked Grandfather casually.

'We can't get into the toilet,' said someone. 'There's a huge snake inside.'

'Let me take a look,' said Grandfather. 'I know all about snakes.'

The passengers made way for him, and he entered the washroom to find the python curled up in the washbasin. After its heavy meal it had become thirsty and, finding the lid of the tiffin basket easy to pry up, had set out in search of water.

Grandfather gathered up the sleepy, overfed python and stepped out of the washroom. The passengers hastily made way for them.

'Nothing to worry about,' said Grandfather cheerfully. 'It's just a harmless young python. He's had his dinner already, so no one is in any danger!' And he marched back to our compartment with the python in his arms. As soon as I was inside, he bolted the door.

Grandmother was sitting up on her berth.

'I knew you'd do something foolish behind my back,' she scolded. 'You told me you'd got rid of that creature, and all the time you've been hiding it from me.'

Grandfather tried to explain that we had nothing to do with it, that the python had smuggled itself into the tiffin basket, but Grandmother was unconvinced. 'What will Mabel do when she sees it!' she cried despairingly.

My Aunt Mabel was a schoolteacher in Lucknow. She was going to share our new house, and she was terrified of all reptiles, particularly snakes.

'We won't let her see it,' said Grandfather. 'Back it goes into the tiffin basket.'

Early next morning, the train steamed into Lucknow. Aunt Mabel was on the platform to receive us.

Grandfather let all the other passengers get off before he emerged from the compartment with Timothy on a chain. I had Chips in my pocket, suitcase in both hands. Popeye stayed perched on Grandmother's shoulder, eyeing the busy platform with considerable distrust.

Aunt Mabel, a lover of good food, immediately spotted the tiffin basket, picked it up and said, 'It's not very heavy. I'll carry it out to the taxi. I hope you've kept something for me.'

'A whole chicken,' I said.

'We hardly ate anything,' said Grandfather.

'It's all yours, Aunty!' I added.

'Oh, good!' exclaimed Aunt Mabel. 'Its been ages since I tasted something cooked by your grandmother.' And after that there was no getting the basket away from her.

Glancing at it, I thought I saw the lid bulging, but Grandfather had tied it down quite firmly this time and there was little likelihood of its suddenly bursting open.

An enormous 1950 Chevrolet taxi was waiting outside the station, and the family tumbled into it. Timothy got onto the back seat, leaving enough room for Grandfather and me. Aunt Mabel sat in front with Grandmother, the tiffin basket on her lap.

'Tell the taxi driver where to take us, dear,' said Grandmother. He's looking rather nervous.'

Aunt Mabel gave instructions to the driver and the taxi shot off in a cloud of dust.

'Well, here we go!' said Grandfather. 'I'm looking forward to settling into the new house.'

Popeye, perched proudly on Grandmother's shoulder, kept one suspicious eye on the quivering tiffin basket.

'All aboard!' he squawked. 'All aboard!'

When we got to our new house, we found a light breakfast waiting for us on the dining table.

'It isn't much,' said Aunt Mabel. 'But we'll supplement it with the contents of your hamper.' And placing the basket on the table, she removed the lid.

The python was half-asleep, with an apple in its mouth. Aunt Mabel was no Eve, to be tempted. She fainted away.

Grandfather promptly picked up the python, took it into the garden, and draped it over a branch of a guava tree.

When Aunt Mabel recovered, she insisted that there was a huge snake in the tiffin basket. We showed her the empty basket.

'You're seeing things,' said Grandfather.

'It must be the heat,' I said.

Grandmother said nothing. But Popeye broke into shrieks of maniacal laughter, and soon everyone, including a slightly hysterical Aunt Mabel, was doubled up with laughter.

Timothy

Timothy, the tiger cub, was discovered by Grandfather on a hunting expedition in the Terai jungle near Dehra.

Grandfather was no shikari, but as he knew the forests of the Siwalik hills better than most people, he was persuaded to accompany the party—it consisted of several Very Important Persons from Delhi—to advise on the terrain and the direction the beaters should take once a tiger had been spotted.

The camp itself was sumptuous—seven large tents (one for each shikari), a dining-tent, and a number of servants' tents. The dinner was very good, as Grandfather admitted afterwards; it was not often that one saw hot-water plates, finger-glasses, and seven or eight courses, in a tent in the jungle! But that was how things were done in the days of the Viceroys . . . There were also some fifteen elephants, four of them with howdahs for the shikaris, and the others specially trained for taking part in the beat.

The sportsmen never saw a tiger, nor did they shoot anything else, though they saw a number of deer, peacocks, and wild boars. They were giving up all hope of finding a tiger, and were beginning to shoot at jackals, when Grandfather, strolling down the forest path at some distance from the rest of the party, discovered a little tiger about eighteen inches long, hiding among the intricate roots of a banyan tree. Grandfather picked him up, and brought him home after the camp had broken up. He had the distinction of being the only member of the party to have bagged any game, dead or alive.

At first the tiger cub, who was named Timothy by Grandmother, was brought up entirely on milk given to him in a feeding bottle by our cook, Mahmoud. But the milk proved too rich for him, and he was put on a diet of raw mutton and cod liver oil, to be followed later by a more tempting diet of pigeons and rabbits.

Timothy was provided with two companions—Toto the monkey, who was bold enough to pull the young tiger by the tail, and then climb up the curtains if Timothy lost his temper; and a small mongrel puppy, found on the road by Grandfather.

At first Timothy appeared to be quite afraid of the puppy, and darted back with a spring if it came too near. He would make absurd dashes at it with his large forepaws, and then retreat to a ridiculously safe distance. Finally, he allowed the puppy to crawl on his back and rest there!

One of Timothy's favourite amusements was to stalk anyone who would play with him, and so, when I came to live with Grandfather, I became one of the favourites of the tiger. With a crafty look in his glittering eyes, and his body crouching, he would creep closer and closer to me, suddenly making a dash for my feet, rolling over on his back and kicking me in delight, and pretending to bite my ankles.

He was by this time the size of a full-grown retriever, and when I took him out for walks, people on the road would give us a wide berth. When he pulled hard on his chain, I had difficulty in keeping up with him. His favourite place in the house was the drawing room, and he would make himself comfortable on the long sofa, reclining there with great dignity, and snarling at anybody who tried to get him off.

Timothy had clean habits, and would scrub his face with his paws exactly like a cat. He slept at night in the cook's quarters, and was always delighted at being let out by him in the morning.

'One of these days,' declared Grandmother in her prophetic manner, 'we are going to find Timothy sitting on Mahmoud's bed, and no sign of the cook except his clothes and shoes!'

Of course, it never came to that, but when Timothy was about six months old a change came over him; he grew steadily less friendly. When out for a walk with me, he would try to steal away to stalk a cat or someone's pet Pekinese. Sometimes at night we would hear frenzied cackling from the poultry house, and in the morning there would be feathers lying all over the veranda. Timothy had to be chained up more often. And finally, when he began to stalk Mahmoud about the house with what looked like villainous intent, Grandfather decided it was time to transfer him to a zoo.

The nearest zoo was at Lucknow, two hundred miles away. Reserving a first-class compartment for himself and Timothy—no one would share a compartment with them—Grandfather took him to Lucknow where the zoo authorities were only too glad to receive as a gift a well-fed and fairly civilized tiger.

About six months later, when my grandparents were visiting their relatives in Lucknow, Grandfather took the opportunity of calling at the zoo to see how Timothy was getting on. I was not there to accompany him, but I heard all about it when he returned to Dehra.

Arriving at the zoo, Grandfather made straight for the particular cage in which Timothy had been interned. The tiger was there, crouched in a corner, full-grown and with a magnificent striped coat.

'Hello Timothy!' said Grandfather, and, climbing the railing with ease, he put his arm through the bars of the cage.

The tiger approached the bars, and allowed Grandfather to put both hands around his head. Grandfather stroked the tiger's forehead and tickled his ear, and whenever he growled, smacked him across the mouth, which was his old way of keeping him quiet.

He licked Grandfather's hands and only sprang away when a leopard in the next cage snarled at him. Grandfather 'shooed' the leopard away, and the tiger returned to lick his hands; but every now and then the leopard would rush at the bars, and the tiger would slink back to his corner.

A number of people had gathered to watch the reunion when a keeper pushed his way through the crowd and asked Grandfather what he was doing.

'I'm talking to Timothy,' said Grandfather. 'Weren't you here when I gave him to the zoo six months ago?'

'I haven't been here very long,' said the surprised keeper. 'Please continue your conversation. But I have never been able to touch him myself, he is always very bad tempered.'

'Why don't you put him somewhere else?' suggested Grandfather. 'That leopard keeps frightening him. I'll go and see the Superintendent about it.'

Grandfather went in search of the Superintendent of the zoo, but found that he had gone home early; and so, after wandering about the zoo for a little while, he returned to Timothy's cage to say goodbye. It was beginning to get dark.

He had been stroking and slapping Timothy for about five minutes when he found another keeper observing him with some alarm. Grandfather recognized him as the keeper who had been there when Timothy had first come to the zoo.

'You remember me,' said Grandfather. 'Now why don't you transfer Timothy to another cage, away from this stupid leopard?'

'But—sir—' stammered the keeper, 'it is not your tiger.'

'I know, I know,' said Grandfather testily. 'I realize he is no longer mine. But you might at least take a suggestion or two from me.'

'I remember your tiger very well,' said the keeper. 'He died two months ago.'

'Died!' exclaimed Grandfather.

'Yes, sir, of pneumonia. This tiger was trapped in the hills only last month, and he is very dangerous!'

Grandfather could think of nothing to say. The tiger was still licking his arm, with increasing relish. Grandfather took what seemed to him an age to withdraw his hand from the cage.

With his face near the tiger's he mumbled, 'Goodnight, Timothy,' and giving the keeper a scornful look, walked briskly out of the zoo.

II

The Civilized Wilderness

Wherever I have lived, be it city or small town or hill station, I have always managed to find some corner where birds sing, or flowers grow, or small creatures survive. Even when I found myself spending a few days in a small ward in a New Delhi nursing home, I discovered that there were pigeons living in the skylight. They made me feel that I still belonged to the world outside.

Live close to nature and you will never feel lonely. Don't drive those sparrows out of your veranda; they won't hack into your computer.

Firefly In My Room

Last night, as I lay sleepless
In the summer dark
With window open to invite a breeze,
Softly a firefly flew in
And circled round the room
Twinkling at me from floor or wall
Or ceiling, never long in one place,
But lighting up little spaces . . .
A friendly presence, dispelling
The settled gloom of an unhappy day.

And after it had gone, I left
The window open, just in case
It should return.

The Good Earth

As with many who love gardens, I have never really
had enough space in which to create a proper
garden of my own. A few square feet of rocky

hillside has been the largest patch at my disposal. All that I managed to grow on it were daisies—and they'd probably have grown there anyway. Still, they made for a charmingly dappled hillside throughout the summer, especially on full moon nights when the flowers were at their most radiant.

For the past few years, here in Mussoorie, I have had to live in two small rooms on the second floor of a tumbledown building which has no garden space at all. All the same, it has a number of ever-widening cracks in which wild sorrels, dandelions, thornapples and nettles all take root and thrive. You could, I suppose, call it a wild wall-garden. Not that I am deprived of flowers. I am better off than most city dwellers because I have only to walk a short way out of the hill station to see (or discover) a variety of flowers in their wild state; and wild flowers are rewarding, because the best ones are often the most difficult to find.

But I have always had this dream of possessing a garden of my own. Not a very formal garden—certainly not the 'stately home' type, with its pools and fountains and neat hedges as described in such detail by Bacon in his essay 'Of Gardens'. Bacon had a methodical mind, and he wanted a methodical garden. I like a garden to be a little untidy, unplanned, full of surprises—rather like my own muddled mind, which gives even me a few surprises at times.

My grandmother's garden in Dehra, in north

India, for example; Grandmother liked flowers, and she didn't waste space on lawns and hedges. There was plenty of space at the back of the house for shrubs and fruit trees, but the front garden was a maze of flower beds of all shapes and sizes, and everything that could grow in Dehra (a fertile valley) was grown in them—masses of sweet peas, petunias, antirrhinum, poppies, phlox, and larkspur; scarlet poinsettia leaves draped the garden walls, while purple and red bougainvillea climbed the porch; geraniums of many hues mounted the veranda steps; and, indoors, vases full of cut flowers gave the rooms a heady fragrance. I suppose it was this garden of my childhood that implanted in my mind the permanent vision of a perfect garden so that, whenever I am worried or down in the dumps, I close my eyes and conjure up a picture of this lovely place, where I am wandering through forests of cosmos and banks of rambling roses. It soothes the agitated mind.

I remember an aunt who sometimes came to stay with my grandmother, and who had an obsession about watering the flowers. She would be at it morning and evening, an old and rather lopsided watering-can in her frail hands. To everyone's amazement, she would water the garden in all weathers, even during the rains.

'But it's just been raining, aunt,' I would remonstrate. Why are you watering the garden?'

'The rain comes from above,' she would reply. 'This is from me. They expect me at this time, you know.'

Grandmother died when I was still a boy, and the garden soon passed into other hands. I've never done well enough to be able to acquire something like it. And there's no point in getting sentimental about the past.

Yes, I'd love to have a garden of my own—spacious and gracious, and full of everything that's fragrant and flowering. But if I don't succeed, never mind—I've still got the dream.

I wouldn't go so far as to say that a garden is the answer to all problems, but it's amazing how a little digging and friendly dialogue with the good earth can help reactivate us when we grow sluggish.

Before I moved into my present home which has no space for a garden, I had, as I've said, a tiny patch on a hillside, where I grew some daisies. Whenever I was stuck in the middle of a story or an essay, I would go into my tiny hillside garden and get down to the serious business of transplanting or weeding or pruning or just plucking off dead blooms, and in no time at all I was struck with a notion of how to proceed with the stalled story, reluctant essay, or unresolved poem.

Not all gardeners are writers, but you don't have to be a writer to benefit from the goodness of your garden. Baldev, who heads a large business corporation in Delhi, tells me that he wouldn't dream of going to his office unless he'd spent at least half an hour in his garden that morning. If you can start the day by looking at the dew on your antirrhinums, he tells me, you can face the stormiest of board meetings.

Or take Cyril, an old friend.

When I met him, he was living in a small apartment on the first floor of a building that looked over a steep, stony precipice. The house itself appeared to be built on stilts, although these turned out to be concrete pillars. Altogether an ugly edifice. 'Poor Cyril,' I thought. 'There's no way *he* can have a garden.'

I couldn't have been more wrong. Cyril's rooms were surrounded by a long veranda that allowed in so much sunlight and air, resulting in such a profusion of leaf and flower, that at first I thought I was back in one of the greenhouses at Kew Gardens, where I used to wander during a lonely sojourn in London.

Cyril found a chair for me among the tendrils of a climbing ivy, while a coffee table materialized from behind a plant. By the time I had recovered enough from taking in my arboreal surroundings, I discovered that there were at least two other guests— one concealed behind a tree-sized philodendron, the other apparently embedded in a pot of begonias.

Cyril, of course, was an exception. We cannot

all have sunny verandas; nor would I show the same tolerance as he does towards the occasional caterpillar on my counterpane. But he was a happy man until his landlord, who lived below, complained that water was cascading down through the ceiling.

'Fix the ceiling,' said Cyril, and went back to watering his plants. It was the end of a beautiful tenant–landlord relationship.

So let us move on to the washerwoman who lives down the road, a little distance from my own abode. She and her family live at the subsistence level. They have one square meal at midday, and they keep the leftovers for the evening. But the steps to their humble quarters are brightened by geraniums potted in large tin cans, all ablaze with several shades of flower.

Hard as I try, I cannot grow geraniums to match hers. Does she scold her plants the way she scolds her children? Maybe I'm not firm enough with my geraniums. Or has it something to do with the washing? Anyway, her abode certainly looks more attractive than some of the official residences here in Mussoorie.

Some gardeners like to specialize in particular flowers, but specialization has its dangers. My friend, Professor Saili, an ardent admirer of the nature poetry of William Wordsworth, decided he would have his own field of nodding daffodils, and planted daffodil bulbs all over his front yard. The following spring, after much waiting, he was rewarded by the appearance of a solitary daffodil that looked like a railway passenger who had gotten off at the wrong station. This year he is specializing in 'easy-to-grow' French marigolds. They grow easily enough in France, I'm sure; but the professor is discovering that they are stubborn growers on our stony Himalayan soil.

Not everyone in this hill station has a lovely garden. Some palatial homes and spacious hotels are approached through forests of weeds, clumps of nettle, and dead or dying rose bushes. The owners are often plagued by personal problems that prevent them from noticing the state of their gardens. Loveless lives, unloved gardens.

On the other hand, there was Annie Powell, who, at the age of ninety, was up early every morning to water her lovely garden. Watering-can in hand, she would move methodically from one flower bed to the next, devotedly giving each plant a sprinkling. She said she loved to see leaves and flowers sparkling with fresh water, it gave her a new lease of life every day.

And there were my maternal grandparents, whose home in Dehra in the valley was surrounded by a beautiful, well-kept garden. How I wish I had been old enough to prevent that lovely home from passing into other hands. But no one can take away our memories.

Grandfather looked after the orchard,

Grandmother looked after the flower garden. Like all people who have lived together for many years, they had the occasional disagreement.

Grandfather would proceed to sulk on a bench beneath the jackfruit tree while, at the other end of the garden, Grandmother would start clipping a hedge with more than her usual vigour. Silently, imperceptibly, they would make their way toward the centre of the garden, where the flower beds gave way to a vegetable patch. This was neutral ground. My cousins and I looked on like UN observers. And there among the cauliflowers, conversation would begin again, and the quarrel would be forgotten. There's nothing like home-grown vegetables for bringing two people together.

Red roses for young lovers. French beans for longstanding relationships!

A Wilderness in New Delhi

If you are determined, you can find a wilderness close to you, no matter where you live. In 1959, I was living on the outskirts of a greater, further New Delhi. The influx of refugees from the Punjab after Partition had led to many new colonies springing up on the outskirts of the capital, and at the time the furthest of these was Rajouri Garden. Needless to say, there were no gardens. The treeless colony was buffeted by hot, dusty winds from Haryana and Rajasthan. The houses were built on one side of the Najafgarh Road. On the other side, as yet uncolonized, were extensive fields of wheat and other crops still belonging to the original inhabitants. In an attempt to escape the city life that constantly oppressed me, I would walk across the main road and into the fields, finding old wells, irrigation channels, camels and buffaloes, and sighting birds and small creatures that no longer dwelt in the city. In an odd way, it was my reaction to city life that led to my taking a greater interest in the natural world. Up to that time, I had taken it all for granted.

The notebook I kept at the time lies before me now, and my first entry describes the bluejays or rollers that were so much a feature of those remaining open spaces. At rest, the bird is fairly nondescript, but when it takes flight it reveals the glorious bright blue wings and the tail, banded with a lighter blue. It sits motionless, but the large dark eyes are constantly watching the ground in every direction. A grasshopper or cricket has only to make a brief appearance, and the bluejay will launch itself straight at its prey. In spring and early summer the 'roller' lives up to its other name. It indulges in love flights in which it rises and falls in the air with harsh grating screams—a real rock-'n'-roller!

Some way down the Najafgarh Road was a large village pond and beside it a magnificent banyan tree. We have no place for banyan trees today, they need so much space in which to spread their limbs and live comfortably. Cut away its aerial roots and the great tree topples over—usually to make way for a spacious apartment building. That was the first banyan tree I got to know well. It had about a hundred pillars supporting the boughs, and above them there was this great leafy crown like a pillared hall. It has been said that whole armies could shelter in the shade of an old banyan. And probably at one time they did. I saw another sort of army visit the banyan by the village pond when it was in fruit. Parakeets, mynas, rosy pastors, crested bulbuls without crests, barbets and many other birds crowded the tree in order to feast noisily on big, scarlet figs.

Even further down the Najafgarh Road was a large jheel, famous for its fishing. I wonder if any part of the jheel still exists, or if it got filled in and became a part of greater Delhi. One could rest in the shade of a small babul or keekar tree and watch the kingfisher skim over the water, making just a slight splash as it dived and came up with small glistening fish. Our common Indian kingfisher is a beautiful little bird with a brilliant blue back, a white throat and orange underparts. I would spot one perched on an overhanging bush or rock, and wait to see it plunge like an arrow into the water and return to its perch to devour the catch. It came over the water in a flash of gleaming blue, shrilling its loud 'tit-tit-tit'.

The kingfisher is the subject of a number of legends, and the one I remember best, recounted by Romain Rolland, tells us that it was originally a plain grey bird that acquired its resplendent colours by flying straight towards the sun when Noah let it out of the Ark. Its upper plumage took the colour of the sky above, while the lower was scorched a deep russet by the rays of the setting sun.

Summer and winter, I scorned the dust and the traffic, and walked all over Delhi, in search of quiet spots with some shade, a few birds, flower and fruit. I spent many afternoons lying on the grass near India Gate and eating jamuns. I liked the sour tang of the jamun fruit which was best eaten with a little salt. And I liked the deep purple colour of the fruit. Jamuns were one of the nicer things about Delhi.

A Bush at Hand Is Good for Many a Bird

The thing I like most about shrubs and small bushes is that they are about my size or thereabouts. I can meet them on equal terms. Most trees grow tall, they overtake us after a few years, and we find ourselves looking up to them with a certain amount of awe and deference. And so we should.

A bush, on the other hand, may have been in the ground a long time—thirty or forty years or more—while continuing to remain a bush, man-sized and approachable. A bush may spread sideways or gain in substance, but it seldom towers over you. This means that I can be on intimate terms with it, know its qualities—of leaf, bud, flower, and fruit—and also its inhabitants, be they insects, birds, small mammals, or reptiles.

Of course, we know that bushes are ideal for binding the earth together and preventing erosion. In this respect they are just as important as trees. Every monsoon I witness landslides all about me, but I know the hillside just above my cottage is well-knit, knotted and netted, by bilberry and raspberry, wild jasmine, dog-rose and bramble, and other shrubs, vines, and creepers.

I have made a small bench in the middle of this civilized wilderness. And sitting here, I can look down on my own roof, as well as sideways and upward, into a number of bushes, teeming with life throughout the year. This is my favourite place. No one can find me here, unless I call out and make my presence known. The buntings and sparrows, 'grown accustomed to my face' and welcoming the grain I scatter for them, flit about near my feet. One of them, bolder than the rest, alights on my shoe and proceeds to polish his beak on the leather. The sparrows are here all the year round. So are the whistling-thrushes, who live in the shadows between house and hill, sheltered by a waterwood bush, so cared because it likes cool, damp places.

Summer brings the fruit-eating birds, for now that the berries are ripe, a pair of green pigeons, rare in these parts, scramble over the branches of a hawthorn bush, delicately picking off the fruit. The raspberry bush is raided by bands of finches and greedy yellow-bottomed bulbuls. A flock of bright green parrots comes swooping down on the medlar tree, but they do not stay for long. Taking flight at my approach, they wheel above, green and gold in the sunlight, and make for the plum trees further down the road.

The kingora, a native Himalayan shrub similar to the bilberry, attracts small boys as well as birds. On their way to and from school, the boys scramble up the hillside and help themselves to the small sweet and sour berries. Then, lips stained purple, they go their merry way. The birds return.

Other inhabitants of this shrub-land include the skink, a tiny lizard-like reptile, quite harmless. It emerges from its home among stones or roots to sun itself or drink from a leaf-cup of water. I have to protect these skinks from a large prowling tabby cat who thinks the hillside and everything on it belong to him. From my bench, I can see him move stealthily around the corner of my roof. He has his eye on the slow-moving green pigeons. I shall have to watch out for him. There wouldn't be much point in encouraging the birds to visit my bushes if the main beneficiary is to be that handsome, but singleminded cat!

There are flowering shrubs, too—a tangle of dog-roses, the wild yellow jasmine, a buddleia popular with honey bees, and a spreading mayflower which today is covered with small saffron-winged butterflies.

The grass, straw-yellow in winter, is now green and sweet, sprinkled with buttercups and clover. I can abandon the bench and lie on the grass, studying it at close quarters while repeating Whitman's lines:

A child said 'What is the grass?' fetching it
to me with full hands.
How could I answer the child? I do not
know what it is any more than he.

I am no wiser, either, but grass is obviously a good thing, providing a home for crickets and ladybirds and other small creatures. It wouldn't be much fun living on a planet where grass could not grow.

That cat agrees with me. He is flat on his stomach on the grass, inching closer to one of those defenceless little skinks. He has decided that a skink in hand is worth two birds in a bush. I get to my feet, and the cat runs away.

The green pigeons have also flown away. The

smaller birds remain where they are; they know they are too swift for the prowler. I return to my bench and watch the finches and coppersmiths arrive and depart.

You might call my shrubbery an arrival and departure lounge for small birds, but they are also free to take up residence if they wish. Their presence adds sweetness to my life. A bush at hand is good for many a bird.

Zone for Dancing

No night is so dark as it seems.

Here in Landour, on the first range of the Himalayas, I have grown accustomed to the night's brightness—moonlight, starlight, lamplight, firelight! Even fireflies light up the darkness.

Over the years, the night has become my friend. On the one hand, it gives me privacy; on the other, it provides me with limitless freedom.

Not many people relish the dark. There are some who will even sleep with their lights burning all night. They feel safer that way. Safer from the phantoms conjured up by their imaginations. A primeval instinct, perhaps, going back to the time when primitive man hunted by day and was in turn hunted by night.

And yet, I have always felt safer by night, provided I do not deliberately wander about on cliff tops or roads where danger is known to lurk. It's true that burglars and lawbreakers often work by night, their principal object being to get into other people's houses and make off with the silver or the family jewels. They are not into communing with the stars. Nor are late-night revellers, who are usually to be found in brightly lit places and are thus easily avoided. The odd drunk stumbling home is quite harmless and probably in need of guidance.

I feel safer by night, yes, but then I do have the advantage of living in the mountains, in a region where crime and random violence are comparatively rare. I know that if I were living in a big city in some other part of the world, I would think twice about walking home at midnight, no matter how pleasing the night sky would be.

Walking home at midnight in Landour can be quite eventful, but in a different sort of way. One is conscious all the time of the silent life in the surrounding trees and bushes. I have smelt a leopard without seeing it. I have seen jackals on the prowl. I have watched foxes dance in the moonlight. I have seen flying squirrels flit from one treetop to another. I have observed pine martens on their nocturnal journeys, and listened to the calls of nightjars and owls and other birds who live by night.

Not all on the same night, of course. That would be a case of too many riches all at once. Some night walks can be uneventful. But usually there is something to see or hear or sense. Like those foxes dancing in the moonlight. One night, when I got home, I sat down and wrote these lines:

> As I walked home last night,
> I saw a lone fox dancing
> In the bright moonlight.
> I stood and watched; then
> Took the low road, knowing
> The night was his by right.
> Sometimes, when words ring true,
> I'm like a lone fox dancing
> In the morning dew.

Who else, apart from foxes, flying squirrels and night-loving writers are at home in the dark? Well, there are the nightjars, not much to look at, although their large, lustrous eyes gleam uncannily in the light of a lamp. But their sounds are distinctive. The breeding call of the Indian nightjar resembles the sound of a stone skimming over the surface of a frozen pond; it can be heard for a considerable distance. Another species utters a loud grating call which, when close at hand, sounds exactly like a whiplash cutting the air. 'Horsfield's nightjar' (with which I am more familiar in Mussoorie) makes a noise similar to that made by striking a plank with a hammer.

I must not forget the owls, those most celebrated of night birds, much maligned by those who fear the night. Most owls have very pleasant calls. The little jungle owlet has a note which is both mellow and musical. One misguided writer has likened its call to a motorcycle starting up, but this is libel. If only motorcycles sounded like the jungle owl, the world would be a more peaceful place to live and sleep in.

Then there is the little scops owl, who speaks only in monosyllables, occasionally saying 'wow' softly but with great deliberation. He will continue to say 'wow' at intervals of about a minute, for several hours throughout the night.

Probably the most familiar of Indian owls is the spotted owlet, a noisy bird who pours forth a volley of chuckles and squeaks in the early evening and at intervals all night. Towards sunset, I watch the owlets emerge from their holes one after another. Before coming out, each puts out a queer little round head with staring eyes. After they have emerged they usually sit very quietly for a time as though only half awake. Then, all of a sudden, they begin to chuckle, finally breaking out in a torrent of chattering. Having in this way 'psyched' themselves into the right frame of mind, they spread their short, rounded wings and sail off for the night's hunting.

And I wend my way homewards. 'Night with her train of stars' is always enticing. The poet Henley found her so. But he also wrote of 'her great gift of sleep', and it is this gift that I am now about to accept with gratitude and humility.

A Village in the Mountains

I wake to what sounds like the din of a factory buzzer but is in fact the music of a single vociferous cicada in the lime tree near my bed.

We have slept out of doors. I wake at first light, focus on a pattern of small, glossy leaves, and then through them see the mountains, the mighty Himalayas, striding away into an immensity of the sky.

'In a thousand ages of the gods I could not tell thee of the glories of Himachal,' so confessed a poet at the dawn of Indian history, and no one since has been able to do real justice to the Himalayas. We have climbed their highest peaks, but still the mountains remain remote, mysterious, primeval.

No wonder, then, that the people who live on these mountain slopes, in the mist-filled valleys of Garhwal, have long since learned humility, patience, and a quiet reserve.

I am their guest for a few days. My friend, Gajadhar, has brought me to his home, to his village above the little Nayar river. We took a train up to the foothills and then we took a bus, and when we were in the hills we walked until we came to this village called Manjari clinging to the terraced slopes of a very proud mountain.

It is my fourth morning in the village. Other mornings I was being awakened by the throaty chuckles of the redbilled blue magpies, but today the cicada has drowned all birdsong.

Early though it is, I am the last to get up. Gajadhar is exercising in the courtyard. He has a fine physique, with the sturdy legs that most Garhwalis possess. I am sure he will realize his ambition of getting into the army. His younger brother, Chakradhar, a slim fair youth, is milking the family's buffalo. Their mother is lighting a fire. She is a handsome woman, although her ears, weighed down by heavy silver earrings, have lost their natural shape. The smaller children, a boy and a girl, are getting ready for school. Their father is in the army, and he is away for most of the year. Gajadhar has been going to a college in the plains, but his mother, with the help of Chakradhar, manages to look after the fields, the house, the goats, and the buffalo. There are spring sowings of corn, monsoon ploughings, September harvestings of rice, and then again autumn sowings of wheat and barley.

They depend on rainfall here, as the village is far above the river. The monsoon is still a month away, but there must be water for cooking, washing, and drinking, and this has to be fetched from the river. And so, after a glass each of hot buffalo's milk, the two brothers and I set off down a rough track to the river.

The sun has climbed the mountains but it has yet to reach the narrow valley. We bathe in the river. Gajadhar and Chakradhar dive in off a massive rock, but I wade in circumspectly, unfamiliar with the river's depth and currents. The water, a milky blue, comes from the melting snows and is very cold. I bathe quickly and then dash for a strip of sand where a little sunshine has now spilt down the mountain in warm, golden pools of light.

A little later, buckets filled, we toil up the steep mountainside. A different way this time. We have to take the proper path if we are not to come tumbling down with our pails of water. The path leads up past the school, a small temple, and a single shop in which it is possible to buy soap, salt, and a few other necessities. It is also the post office.

The postman is yet to arrive. The mail is brought in relays from Lansdowne, about thirty miles away. So, later in the day, Gajadhar and I trek to a bigger post office outside the village. Gajadhar has been walking there and back almost every day, anxious for a letter. He is expecting the result of his army entrance exam. If he is successful, he will be called for an interview. And then, if he makes a good impression, he will be given training as an officer cadet!

As we pass the small village school, the children, who have been having a break, crowd round us, eager to have a glimpse of me. They have never seen a white face before. The adults had dealt with British officials in the 1940s but it is over twenty years since a European stepped into the village. I am the cynosure of all eyes. The children exclaim, point at me with delight, chatter among themselves. I might be a visitor from another planet instead of just an itinerant writer from the plains.

We are rewarded at the end of our trek— Gajadhar gets his letter. He has passed his exam, and will leave with me in the morning. We hurry back. We have to be up early the next morning to complete the thirty-mile trek to Lansdowne in a single day. And so, after an evening with friends, and a partridge for dinner (a present from a neighbour who thinks Gajadhar will make a fine husband for his comely daughter), we retire to our beds: I, to my cot under the lime tree. The moon has not yet risen and the cicadas are silent.

I stretch myself out on the cot under a sky brilliant with stars. And as I close my eyes someone brushes against the lime tree, bruising its leaves, and the good fresh fragrance of lime comes to me on the night air, making that moment memorable for all time.

The Beetle Who Blundered In

When mist fills the Himalayan valleys, and heavy monsoon rain sweeps across the hills, it is natural for wild creatures to seek shelter. Any shelter is welcome in a storm—and sometimes my cottage in the forest is the most convenient refuge.

There is no doubt that I make things easier for all concerned by leaving most of my windows open—I am one of those peculiar people who like to have plenty of fresh air indoors—and if a few birds, beasts and insects come in too, they're welcome, provided they don't make too much of a nuisance of themselves.

I must confess that I did lose patience with a bamboo beetle who blundered in the other night and fell into the water jug. I rescued him and pushed him out of the window. A few seconds later he came whirring in again, and with unerring accuracy landed with a plop in the same jug. I fished him out once more and offered him the freedom of the night. But attracted no doubt by the light and warmth of my small sitting room, he came buzzing back, circling the room like a helicopter looking for a good place to land. Quickly I covered the water jug. He landed in a bowl of wild dahlias, and I allowed him to remain there, comfortably curled up in the hollow of a flower.

Sometimes, during the day, a bird visits me—a deep purple whistling-thrush, hopping about on long dainty legs, peering to right and left, too nervous to sing. She perches on the window sill, looking out at the rain. She does not permit any familiarity. But if I sit quietly in my chair, she will sit quietly on her window sill, glancing quickly at me now and then just to make sure that I'm keeping my distance. When the rain stops, she glides away, and it is only then, confident in her freedom, that she bursts into full-throated song, her broken but haunting melody echoing down the ravine.

A squirrel comes sometimes, when his home in the oak tree gets waterlogged. Apparently he is a bachelor; anyway, he lives alone. He knows me well, this squirrel, and is bold enough to climb on to the dining table looking for tidbits which he always finds, because I leave them there deliberately. Had I met him when he was a youngster, he would have learned to eat from my hand, but I have only been here a few months. I like it this way. I am not looking for pets: these are simply guests.

Last week, as I was sitting down at my desk to write a long-deferred article, I was startled to see an emerald-green praying mantis sitting on my writing pad. He peered up at me with his protruberant glass-bead eyes, and I stared down at him through my reading glasses. When I gave him a prod, he moved off in a leisurely way. Later I found him examining the binding of Whitman's *Leaves of Grass*; perhaps he had found a succulent bookworm. He disappeared for a couple of days, and then I found him on the dressing table, preening himself before the mirror. Perhaps I am doing him an injustice in assuming that he was preening. Maybe he thought he'd met another mantis and was simply trying to make contact. Anyway, he seemed fascinated by his reflection.

Out in the garden, I spotted another mantis, perched on the jasmine bush. Its arms were raised like a boxer's. Perhaps they're a pair, I thought, and went indoors and fetched my mantis and placed him on the jasmine bush, opposite his fellow insect. He did not like what he saw—no comparison with own image!—and made off in a huff.

My most interesting visitor comes at night, when the lights are still burning—a tiny bat who prefers to fly in at the door, should it be open, and will use the window only if there's no alternative. His object in entering the house is to snap up the moths that cluster around the lamps.

All the bats I've seen fly fairly high, keeping near the ceiling as far as possible, and only descending to ear level (my ear level) when they must; but this particular bat flies in low, like a dive bomber, and does acrobatics amongst the furniture, zooming in and out of chair legs and under tables. Once, while careening about the room in this fashion, he passed straight between my legs.

Has his radar gone wrong, I wondered, or is he just plain crazy?

I went to my shelves of *Natural History* and looked up Bats, but could find no explanation for this erratic behaviour. As a last resort, I turned to an ancient volume, Sterndale's *Indian Mammalia* (Calcutta, 1884), and in it, to my delight, I found what I was looking for:

> a bat found near Mussoorie by Captain Hutton, on the southern range of hills at 5500 feet; head and body, 1.4 inch; skims close to the ground, instead of flying high as bats generally do; habitat, Jharipani, N.W. Himalayas.

Apparently the bat was rare even in 1884.

Perhaps I've come across one of the few surviving members of the species: Jharipani is only two miles from where I live. And I feel rather offended that modern authorities should have ignored this tiny bat; possibly they feel that it is already extinct. If so, I'm pleased to have rediscovered it. I am happy that it survives in my small corner of the woods, and I undertake to celebrate it in verse:

Most bats fly high,
Swooping only
To take some insect on the wing;
But there's a bat I know
Who flies so low
He skims the floor,
He does not enter at the window
But flies in at the door,
Does stunts beneath the furniture—
Is his radar wrong,
Or does he just prefer
Being different from other bats?
And when sometimes
He settles upside down
At the foot of my bed,
I let him be.
On lonely nights, even a crazy bat
Is company.

III

Into the Wild

Living in the hills, or near the great forests, or near the sea, does of course make it easier to engage with the natural world. As a boy and then as a young man, a sense of adventure often took me down unknown roads, to experiences that were often memorable. Encounters with the larger animals, such as the leopard, were rare. But in the hills there is always something new waiting for you around the next bend. For at every bend the entire vista is altered, and our perspective changes too. When we walk close to nature, we come to a better understanding of life; for, it is from the natural world that we first emerged and to which we still belong.

How Far Is the River?

Between the boy and the river was a mountain. I was a small boy, and it was a small river, but the mountain was big.

The thickly forested mountain hid the river, but I knew it was there and what it looked like; I had never seen the river with my own eyes, but from the villagers I had heard of it, of the fish in its waters, of its rocks and currents and waterfalls, and it only remained for me to touch the water and know it personally.

I stood in front of our house on the hill opposite the mountain, and gazed across the valley, dreaming of the river. I was barefooted, not because I couldn't afford shoes, but because I felt free with my feet bare, because I liked the feel of warm stones and cool grass, because not wearing shoes saved me the trouble of taking them off.

It was eleven o'clock in the morning and I knew my parents wouldn't be home till evening. There was a loaf of bread I could take with me, and on the way I might find some fruit. Here was the chance I had been waiting for: it would not come again for a long time, because it was seldom that my father and mother visited friends for the entire day. If I came back before dark, they wouldn't know where I had been.

I went into the house and wrapped the loaf of bread in a newspaper. Then I closed all the doors and windows.

The path to the river dropped steeply into the valley, then rose and went round the big mountain. It was frequently used by the villagers, woodcutters, milkmen, shepherds, mule-drivers—but there were no villages beyond the mountain or near the river.

I passed a woodcutter and asked him how far it was to the river. He was a short, powerful man, with a creased and weathered face, and muscles that stood out in hard lumps.

'Seven miles,' he said. 'Why do you want to know?'

'I am going there,' I said.

'Alone?'

'Of course.'

'It will take you three hours to reach it, and then you have to come back. It will be getting dark, and it is not an easy road.'

'But I'm a good walker,' I said, though I had never walked further than the two miles between our house and my school. I left the woodcutter on the path, and continued down the hill.

It was a dizzy, winding path, and I slipped once

or twice and slid into a bush or down a slope of slippery pine needles. The hill was covered with lush green ferns, the trees were entangled in creepers, and a great wild dahlia would suddenly rear its golden head from the leaves and ferns.

Soon I was in the valley, and the path straightened out and then began to rise. I met a girl who was coming from the opposite direction. She held a scythe with which she had been cutting grass, and there were rings in her nose and ears and her arms were covered with heavy bangles. The bangles made music when she moved her wrists. It was as though her hands spoke a language of their own.

'How far is it to the river?' I asked.

The girl had probably never been to the river, or she may have been thinking of another one, because she said, 'Twenty miles,' without any hesitation.

I laughed and ran down the path. A parrot screeched suddenly, flew low over my head, a flash of blue and green. It took the course of the path, and I followed its dipping flight, running until the path rose and the bird disappeared amongst the trees.

A trickle of water came down the hillside, and I stopped to drink. The water was cold and sharp but very refreshing. But I was soon thirsty again. The sun was striking the side of the hill, and the dusty path became hotter, the stones scorching my feet. I was sure I had covered half the distance: I had been walking for over an hour.

Presently I saw another boy ahead of me, driving a few goats down the path.

'How far is the river?' I asked.

He smiled and said, 'Oh, not far, just round the next hill and straight down.'

Feeling hungry, I unwrapped my loaf of bread and broke it in two, offering one half to the boy. We sat on the hillside and ate in silence.

When we had finished, we walked on together and began talking; and talking, I did not notice the smarting of my feet, and the heat of the sun, the distance I had covered and the distance I had yet to cover. But after some time my companion had to take another path, and once more I was on my own.

I missed the village boy; I looked up and down the mountain path but no one else was in sight. My own home was hidden from view by the side of the mountain, and there was no sign of the river, I began to feel discouraged. If someone had been with me, I would not have faltered; but alone, I was conscious of my fatigue and isolation.

But I had come more than half way, and I couldn't turn back; I had to see the river. If I failed, I would always be a little ashamed of the experience. So I walked on, past stone huts and terraced fields, until there were no more fields or huts, only forest and sun and loneliness. There were no men, and no sign of man's influence—only trees and rocks and grass and small flowers—and silence.

The silence was impressive and a little frightening. There was no movement, except for the bending of grass beneath my feet, and the circling of a hawk against the blind blue of the sky.

Then, as I rounded a sharp bend, I heard the sound of water.

I gasped with surprise and happiness, and began to run. I slipped and stumbled, but I kept on running, until I was able to plunge into the snow-cold mountain water.

And the water was blue and white and wonderful.

A Mountain Stream

Early in summer the grass on the hills is still a pale yellowish green, tinged with brown, and that is how it remains until the monsoon rains bring new life to everything that subsists on the stony Himalayan soil. And then, for four months, the greens are deep, dark and emerald bright.

But one day, taking a narrow path that left the dry Mussoorie ridge to link up with Pari Tibba, I ran across a patch of lush green grass, and I knew there had to be water there.

The grass was soft and springy, spotted with the

crimson of small, wild strawberries. Delicate maidenhair, my favourite fern, grew from a cluster of moist, glistening rocks. Moving the ferns a little, I discovered the spring, a freshet of clear sparkling water.

I never cease to wonder at the tenacity of water—its ability to make its way through various strata of rock, zigzagging, back-tracking, finding space, cunningly discovering faults and fissures in the mountain, and sometimes travelling underground for great distances before emerging into the open. Of course, there's no stopping water—no matter how tiny that little trickle, it has to go somewhere!

Like this little spring. At first I thought it was too small to go anywhere, that it would dry up at the edge of the path. Then I discovered that the grass remained soft and green for some distance along the verge, and that there was moisture beneath the grass. This wet stretch ended abruptly; but, on looking further, I saw that it continued on the other side of the path, after briefly going underground again.

I decided to follow its fortunes as it disappeared beneath a tunnel of tall grass and bracken fern. Slithering down a stony slope, I found myself in a small ravine, and there I discovered that my little spring had grown, having been joined by the waters of another spring bubbling up from beneath a patch of primroses.

A short distance away, a spotted forktail stood on a rock, surveying this marriage of the waters. His long, forked tail moved slowly up and down. He paid no attention to me, being totally absorbed in the movements of a water spider. A swift peck, and the spider vanished, completing the bird's breakfast. Thirsty, I cupped my hands and drank a little water. So did the forktail.

There was now a rivulet to follow, and I continued down the ravine until I came to a small pool that was fed not only by my brook (I was already thinking of it as my very own!), but also by a little cascade of water coming down from a rocky ledge. I climbed a little way up the rocks and entered a small cave, in which there was just enough space for crouching down. Water dripped and trickled off its roof and sides. And most wonderful of all, some of these drops created tiny rainbows, for a ray of sunlight had struck through a crevice in the cave roof making the droplets of moisture radiant with all the colours of the spectrum.

When I emerged from the cave, I saw a pair of pine martins drinking at the pool. As soon as they saw me, they were up and away, bounding across the ravine and into the trees.

The brook was now a small stream, but I could not follow it much further, because the hill went into a steep decline and the water tumbled over large, slippery boulders, becoming a waterfall and then a noisy little torrent as it sped toward the valley.

Climbing up the sides of the ravine to the spur of Pari Tibba, I could see the distant silver of a meandering river, the song river, and I knew my little stream was destined to become part of it; and that the river would be joined by another that could be seen slipping over the far horizon, and that their combined waters would enter the great Ganga, further downstream. This mighty river would, in turn, wander over the rich alluvial plains of northern India, finally debauching into the ocean near the Bay of Bengal.

And the ocean, what was it but another droplet in the universe, in the greater scheme of things? No greater than the glistening drop of water that helped start it all, where the grass grows greener around my little spring on the mountain.

Over the years, this brook at the bottom of the hill has become a familiar. From where I live I can always hear its murmur, but I am no longer conscious of the sound except when I return from a trip to the plains.

I have grown so used to the constant music of water that when I leave it behind I feel naked and alone, bereft of my moorings. It is like getting accustomed to the friendly rattle of teacups every morning, and then waking one day to a deathly stillness and a fleeting moment of panic.

Below the house is a forest of oak and maple and rhododendron. The narrow path that first led me to the brook twists its way down through the trees over an open ridge where red sorrel grows wild and then down steeply through a tangle of thorn bushes, creepers and *rangal*-bamboo.

At the bottom of the hill the path leads on to a grassy verge, surrounded by wild rose. The brook runs close by the verge, tumbling over smooth pebbles, over rocks worn yellow with age, on its way to the plains and to the little Song river and finally to the Ganga.

When I first discovered the brook it was April and the wild roses were flowering, small white blossoms lying in clusters. There were still pink and blue primroses on the hill slopes and, an occasional late-flowering rhododendron provided a splash of red against the dark green of the hill.

The spotted forktail, a bird of the Himalayan streams, was much in evidence during those early visits. It moved nimbly over the boulders with a fairy tread and continually wagged its tail. Both of us had a fondness for standing in running water. Once, while I stood in the brook, I saw a snake swim past, a slim brown snake, beautiful and lonely.

In May and June, when the hills are always brown and dry, it remained cool and green near the stream where ferns and long grasses continued to thrive. It was a secluded spot. Few people came here. Sometimes a milkman or a coal-burner would cross the brook on his way to a village; but the nearby hill station's summer visitors had not discovered this haven of wild and green things.

The monkeys—langurs, in fact, with white and silver-grey fur, black faces and long swishing tails—had discovered the place but they kept to the trees and sunlit slopes. They grew quite accustomed to my presence and carried on about their work and play as though I did not exist.

The young ones scuffled and wrestled like boys while their parents attended to each other's toilets, stretching themselves out on the grass, beautiful animals with slim waists and long sinewy legs and tails full of character. They were clean and polite, much nicer than the red monkeys of the plains.

During the rains the brook became a rushing torrent, bushes and small trees were swept away and the friendly murmur of the water became a threatening boom. I did not visit the place too often then. There were leeches in the long grass and they would fasten themselves onto my legs and feast on my blood.

But it was still worthwhile tramping through the forest to feast my eyes on the foliage that sprang up in tropical profusion—soft, spongy moss; great stag-fern on the trunks of trees; mysterious and sometimes evil-looking lilies and orchids; wild dahlias and the climbing convolvulus opening its purple secrets to the morning sun.

When the rains were over, it was October and the birds were in song again. I could lie in the sun on sweet-smelling grass and gaze up through a pattern of oak leaves into a blind-blue heaven. And I would thank my god for leaves and grass and the smell of things, the smell of mint and myrtle and bruised clover, and the touch of things, the touch of grass and air and sky.

And then after a November hailstorm it was winter and I could not lie on the frost-bitten grass. The sound of the brook was the same but I missed the birds; the grey skies came clutching at my heart and the rain and sleet drove me indoors.

It snowed—the snow lay heavy on the branches of the oak trees and piled up in the culverts—and the grass and the ferns and wild flowers were pressed to sleep beneath a cold white blanket: but the brook flowed on, pushing its way through and under the whiteness, towards another spring, another river.

The Leopard

I first saw the leopard when I was crossing the small stream that ran through the forest at the bottom of the hill on which I lived when I first came to Mussoorie. The ravine was so deep that for most of the day it remained in shadow. This encouraged many birds and animals to emerge from cover during the hours of daylight. Few people ever passed that way. It was one of the few natural sanctuaries left near Mussoorie.

Nearly every morning, and sometimes during the day, I heard the cry of the barking deer. And in the evening walking through the forest, I disturbed parties of kaleej pheasants. The birds went gliding into the ravines on open, motionless wings. I saw pine martins and a handsome red fox. I recognized the footprints of a bear.

As I had not come to take anything from the jungle, the birds and animals soon grew accustomed to my face. Or possibly they recognized my footsteps. After some time, my approach did not disturb them. The langurs in the oak and rhododendron trees, for instance, who would at first go leaping through the branches at my approach, now ignored me, as they munched up the tender green shoots of the oak.

But one evening as I passed, I heard them chattering in the trees and I was not the cause of their excitement.

As I crossed the stream and began climbing the hill, the grunting and chattering increased as though the langurs were trying to warn me of some hidden danger. A shower of pebbles came rattling down the steep hillside and I looked up to see a sinewy orange-gold leopard, poised on a rock about twenty feet above me.

It was not looking towards me but had its head thrust attentively forward in the direction of the ravine. It must have sensed my presence because it slowly turned its head and looked down at me. It seemed a little puzzled at my presence there, and when, to give myself courage, I clapped my hands sharply, the leopard sprang away into the thickets making absolutely no sound as it melted into the shadows. I had disturbed the animal in its quest for food. But a little later I heard the quickening cry of a barking deer as it fled through the forest—the hunt was still on.

The leopard, like other members of the cat family, is nearing extinction in India and I was surprised to find one so close to Mussoorie. Probably the deforestation that had been taking place in the surrounding hills had driven the deer into this green valley and the leopard naturally had followed.

It was some weeks before I saw the leopard again although I was often made aware of its presence. A dry rasping cough sometimes gave it away. At times I felt certain that I was being followed. And once when I was late getting home I was startled by a family of porcupines running about in a clearing. I looked around nervously and saw two bright eyes staring at me from a thicket. I stood still, my heart banging away against my ribs. Then the eyes danced away and I realized they were only fireflies.

One day, I found the remains of a barking deer that had been partially eaten. I wondered why the leopard had not hidden the remains of his meal and decided that he had been disturbed while eating. Then, climbing the hill I met a party of shikaris resting beneath the oaks. They asked me if I had seen a leopard. I said I had not. They said they knew there was a leopard in the forest. Leopard skins, they told me, were selling in Delhi at over a thousand rupees each! Of course, there was a ban on the export of its skins but they gave me to understand that there were ways and means . . . I thanked them for their information and moved on, feeling uneasy and disturbed.

The shikaris had seen the carcass of the deer and the leopard's pug marks and they kept coming to the forest. Almost every evening I heard their guns banging away, for they were ready to fire at almost everything.

'There's leopard about,' they told me. 'You should carry a gun.'

'I don't have one,' I said.

There were fewer birds to be seen and even the langurs had moved on. The red fox did not show itself and the pine martins who had earlier become bold, now dashed into hiding at my approach. The smell of one human is like the smell of any other.

I thought no more of the men. My attitude towards them was similar to the attitude of the denizens of the forest—they were men, unpredictable and to be avoided if possible.

One day after crossing the stream, I climbed Pari Tibba, a bleak, scrub-covered hill where no one lived. This was a stiff undertaking because there was no path to the top and I had to scramble up a precipitous rock face with the help of rocks and roots which were apt to come away in my groping hand. But at the top was a plateau with a few pine trees, their upper branches catching the wind and humming softly. There I found the ruins of what must have been the first settlers—just a few piles of rubble now overgrown with weeds, sorrel, dandelion and nettles.

As I walked through the roofless ruins, I was struck by the silence that surrounded me, the absence of birds and animals, the sense of complete desolation. The silence was so absolute that it seemed to be shouting in my ears. But there was something else of which I was becoming increasingly aware—the strong feline odour of one of the cat family. I paused and looked about. I was alone. There was no movement of dry leaf or loose stone. The ruins were, for the most part, open to the sky. Their rotting rafters had collapsed and joined together to form a low passage like the entrance to a mine. This dark cavern seemed to lead down.

The smell was stronger when I approached this spot so I stopped again and waited there wondering if I had discovered the lair of the leopard, wondering if the animal was now at rest after a night's hunt. Perhaps it was crouched there in the dark, watching me, recognizing me, knowing me as a man who walked alone in the forest without a weapon. I like to think that he was there and that he knew me and that he acknowledged my visit in the friendliest way—by ignoring me altogether.

Perhaps I had made him confident—too confident, too careless, too trusting of the human in his midst. I did not venture any further. I did not seek physical contact or even another glimpse of that beautiful sinewy body, springing from rock to rock . . . It was his trust I wanted and I think he gave it to me. But did the leopard, trusting one man, make the mistake of bestowing his trust on others? Did I, by casting out all fear—my own fear and the leopard's protective fear—leave him defenceless?

Because, next day, coming up the path from the stream, shouting and beating their drums, were the shikaris. They had a long bamboo pole across their shoulder and slung from the pole, feet up, head down, was the lifeless body of the leopard. It had been shot in the neck and in the head.

'We told you there was a leopard!' they shouted, in good humour. 'Isn't he a fine specimen?'

'Yes,' I said, 'he was a beautiful leopard.'

I walked home through the silent forest. It was very silent, almost as though the birds and animals knew their trust had been violated.

I remembered the lines of a poem by D.H. Lawrence and as I climbed the steep and lonely path to my home, the words beat out their rhythm in my mind—'There was no room in the world for a mountain lion and me.'

The Glacier

It was a fine sunny morning—oh so many years ago—when we set out to cover the last seven miles to the glacier, Kamal, Anil, Bisnu and I. We were young, hungry for adventure. We had expected this to be a stiff climb, and it was. The last dak bungalow was situated at well over ten thousand feet above sea level, and the ascent was to be fairly gradual.

And suddenly, abruptly, there were no more trees. As the bungalow dropped out of sight, the trees and bushes gave way to short grass and little blue and pink alpine flowers. The snow peaks were close now, ringing us in on every side. We passed waterfalls, cascading hundreds of feet down precipitous rock faces, thundering into the little river. A great golden eagle hovered over us for some time.

'I feel different again,' said Kamal.

'We're very high now,' I said. 'I hope we won't get headaches.'

'I've got one already,' complained Anil. 'Let's have some tea.'

We had left our cooking utensils at the bungalow, expecting to return there for the night, and had brought with us only a few biscuits, chocolate, and a thermos of tea. We finished the tea, and Bisnu scrambled about on the grassy slopes, collecting wild strawberries. They were tiny strawberries, very sweet, and they did nothing to satisfy our appetites. There was no sign of habitation or human life. The only creatures to be found at that height were the gurals—sure-footed mountain goats—and an occasional snow-leopard, or a bear.

We found and explored a small cave, and then turning a bend, came unexpectedly upon the glacier.

The hill fell away and there, confronting us, was a great white field of snow and ice cradled between two peaks that could only have been the abode of the gods. We were speechless for several minutes. Kamal took my hand and held on to it for reassurance; perhaps he was not sure that what he saw was real. Anil's mouth hung open. Bisnu's eyes glittered with excitement.

We proceeded cautiously on to the snow, supporting each other on the slippery surface, but we could not go far, because we were quite unequipped for any high-altitude climbing. It was pleasant to feel that we were the only boys in our town who had climbed so high. A few black rocks jutted out from the snow, and we sat down on them, to feast our eyes on the view. The sun reflected sharply from the snow, and we felt surprisingly warm.

'Let's sunbathe!' said Anil, on a sudden impulse.

'Yes, let's do that!' I said.

In a few minutes we had taken off our clothes and, sitting on the rocks, were exposing ourselves to the elements. It was delicious to feel the sun crawling over my skin. Within half an hour I was post-box red, and so was Bisnu, and the two of us decided to get into our clothes before the sun scorched the skin off our backs. Kamal and Anil appeared to be more resilient to sunlight, and laughed at our discomfiture. Bisnu and I avenged ourselves by gathering up handfuls of snow and rubbing it on their backs. They dressed quickly enough after that, Anil leaping about like a performing monkey.

Meanwhile, almost imperceptibly, clouds had covered some of the peaks, and a white mist drifted down the mountain slopes. It was time to get back to the bungalow; we would barely make it before dark.

We had not gone far when lightning began to sizzle above the mountain tops, followed by waves of thunder.

'Let's run!' shouted Anil. 'We can take shelter in the cave!'

The clouds could hold themselves in no longer, and the rain came down suddenly, stinging our faces as it was whipped up by an icy wind. Half-blinded, we ran as fast as we could along the slippery path, and stumbled, drenched and exhausted, into the little cave.

The cave was mercifully dry, and not very dark. We remained at the entrance, watching the rain sweep past us, listening to the wind whistling down the long gorge.

'It will take some time to stop,' said Kamal.

'No, it will pass soon,' said Bisnu. 'These storms are short and fierce.'

Anil produced his pocket knife, and to pass the time we carved our names in the smooth rock of the cave.

'We will come here again, when we are older,' said Kamal, 'and perhaps our names will still be here.'

It had grown dark by the time the rain stopped. A full moon helped us find our way. We went slowly and carefully. The rain had loosened the earth and stones kept rolling down the hillside. I was afraid of sporting a landslide.

'I hope we don't meet the Lidini now,' said Anil fervently.

'I thought you didn't believe in her,' I said.

'I don't,' replied Anil. 'But what if I'm wrong?'

We saw only a gural, poised on the brow of a precipice, silhouetted against the sky.

And then the path vanished.

Had it not been for the bright moonlight, we might have walked straight into an empty void. The rain had caused a landslide, and where there had been a narrow path there was now only a precipice of loose, slippery shale.

'We'll have to go back,' said Bisnu. 'It will be too dangerous to try and cross in the dark.'

'We'll sleep in the cave,' I suggested.

'We've nothing to sleep in,' said Anil. 'Not a single blanket between us—and nothing to eat!'

'We'll just have to rough it till morning,' said Kamal. 'It will be better than breaking our necks here.'

We returned to the cave, which did at least have the virtue of being dry. Bisnu had matches, and he made a fire with some dry sticks which had been left in the cave by a previous party. We ate what was left of a loaf of bread.

There was no sleep for any of us that night. We lay close to each other for comfort, but the ground was hard and uneven. And every noise we heard outside the cave made us think of leopards and bears and even Abominable Snowmen.

We got up as soon as there was a faint glow in the sky. The snow peaks were bright pink, but we were too tired and hungry and worried to care for the beauty of the sunrise. We took the path to the landslide, and once again looked for a way across. Kamal ventured to take a few steps on the loose pebbles, but the ground gave way immediately, and we had to grab him by the arms and shoulders to prevent him from sliding a hundred feet down the gorge.

'Now what are we going to do?' I asked.

'Look for another way,' said Bisnu.

'But do you know of any?'

And we all turned to look at Bisnu, expecting him to provide the solution to our problem.

'I have heard of a way,' said Bisnu, 'but I have never used it. It will be a little dangerous, I think. The path has not been used for several years—not since the traders stopped coming in from Tibet.'

'Never mind, we'll try it,' said Anil.

'We will have to cross the glacier first,' said Bisnu. 'That's the main problem.'

We looked at each other in silence. The glacier didn't look difficult to cross, but we knew that it would not be easy for novices. For almost two furlongs it consisted of hard, slippery ice.

Anil was the first to arrive at a decision.

'Come on,' he said. 'There's no time to waste.'

We were soon on the glacier. And we remained on it for a long time. For every two steps forward, we slid one step backward. Our progress was slow and awkward. Sometimes, after advancing several yards across the ice at a steep incline, one of us would slip back and the others would have to slither down to help him up. At one particularly difficult spot, I dropped our water bottle and grabbing at it, lost my footing, fell full-length and went sliding some twenty feet down the ice slope.

I had sprained my wrist and hurt my knee and was to prove a liability for the rest of the trek.

Kamal tied his handkerchief round my hand, and Anil took charge of the water bottle, which we had filled with ice. Using my good hand to grab Bisnu's legs whenever I slipped, I struggled on behind the others.

It was almost noon and we were quite famished, when we put our feet on grass again. And then we had another steep climb, clutching at roots and grasses, before we reached the path that Bisnu had spoken about. It was little more than a goat-track, but it took us round the mountain and brought us within sight of the dak bungalow.

'I could eat a whole chicken,' said Kamal.

'I could eat two,' I said.

'I could eat a Snowman,' said Bisnu.

'And I could eat the chowkidar,' said Anil.

Fortunately for the chowkidar, he had anticipated our hunger, and when we staggered into the bungalow late in the afternoon, we found a meal waiting for us. True, there was no chicken—but, so ravenous did we feel, that even the lowly onion tasted delicious!

We had Bisnu to thank for getting us back successfully. He had brought us over mountain and glacier with all the skill and confidence of a boy who had the Himalayas in his blood.

We took our time getting back to Kapkote. We fished in the Sarayu river, bathed with the village boys we had seen on our way up, collected strawberries and ferns and wild flowers, and finally said goodbye to Bisnu.

Anil wanted to take Bisnu along with us, but the boy's parents refused to let him go, saying that he was too young for the life in a city; but we were of the opinion that Bisnu could have taught the city boys a few things.

'Never mind,' said Kamal. 'We'll go on another trip next year, and we'll take you with us, Bisnu. We'll write and let you know our plans.'

This promise made Bisnu happy, and he saw us off at the bus stop, shouldering our bedding to the end. Then he skimmed up the trunk of a fir tree to have a better view of us leaving, and we saw him waving to us from the tree as our bus went round

the bend from Kapkote, and the hills were left
behind and the plains stretched out below.

The Open Road

As the years go by, I do not walk as far or as fast
as I used to; but speed and distance were never my
forte. Like J. Krishnamurti, I believe that the journey
is more important than the destination. But, then, I
have never really had a destination. The glory that
comes from conquering the Himalayan peaks is not
for me. My greatest pleasure lies in taking path—
any old path will do—and following it until it leads
me to a forest glade or village or stream or windy
hilltop.

This sort of tramping (it does not even qualify
as trekking) is a compulsive thing with me. You
could call it my vice, since it is stronger than the
desire for wine, women or song. To get on to the
open road fills me with joie de vivre, gives me an
exhilaration not found in other, possibly more
worthy, pursuits.

Only this afternoon I had one of my more
enjoyable tramps. I had been cooped up in my room
for several days, while outside it rained and hailed

and snowed and the wind blew icily from all directions. It seemed ages since I'd taken a long walk. Fed up with it all, I pulled on my overcoat, banged the door shut and set off up the hillside.

I kept to the main road, but because of the heavy snow there were no vehicles on it. Even as I walked, flurries of snow struck my face, and collected on my coat and head. Up at the top of the hill, the deodars were clothed in a mantle of white. It was fairyland: everything still and silent. The only movement was the circling of an eagle over the trees. I walked for an hour, and passed only one person, the milkman on his way back to his village. His cans were crowned with snow. He looked a little tipsy. He asked me the time, but before I could tell him he shook me by the hand and said I was a good fellow because I never complained about the water in the milk. I told him that as long as he used clean water, I'd contain my wrath.

On my way back, I passed a small group. It consisted of a person in some sort of uniform (because of the snow I couldn't really make it out), who was hurling epithets at several small children who were busy throwing snowballs at him. He kept shouting: 'Do you know who I am? Do you know who I am?' The children did not want to know. They were only interested in hitting their target, and succeeded once in every five or six attempts.

I came home exhilarated and immediately sat

down beside the stove to write this piece. I found some lines of Stevenson's which seemed appropriate:

And this shall be for music when no one else is near,
The fine song for singing, the rare song to hear!
That only I remember, that only you admire,
Of the broad road that stretches, and the roadside fire.

He speaks directly to me, across the mists of time: R.L. Stevenson, prince of essayists. There is none like him today. We hurry, hurry in a heat of hope—and who has time for roadside fires, except, perhaps, those who must work on the roads in all weathers?

Whenever I walk into the hills, I come across gangs of road-workers breaking stones, cutting into the rocky hillsides, building retaining walls. I am not against more roads—especially in the hills, where the people have remained impoverished largely because of the inaccessibility of their villages. Besides, a new road is one more road for me to explore, and in the interests of progress I am prepared to put up with the dust raised by the occasional bus. And if if becomes too dusty, one can always leave the main road. There is no dearth of paths leading off into the valleys.

On one such diversionary walk, I reached a village where I was given a drink of curds and a meal of rice and beans. That is another of the attractions of tramping to nowhere in particular—the finding of somewhere in particular, the striking up of friendships, the discovery of new springs and waterfalls, unusual plants, rare flowers, strange birds. In the hills, a new vista opens up at every bend in the road.

That is what makes me a compulsive walker—new vistas, and the charm of the unexpected.

IV
Foothill to Treeline

As you ascend the foothills, and then the temperate zones, and then even higher, the flora changes dramatically. At every thousand feet you will find a difference in the trees, shrubs and wild flowers that clothe the hills. And with them a difference in the kind of birds, animals, insects and other creatures that depend on the flora. Here I take you on a brief journey into the mountains, to give you some idea of the variety and richness of our forest wealth.

Trekking Up the Himalayas

India, still rich in flora, is nowhere so prolific as in the eastern and western Himalayas. The mountain slopes and valleys present remarkable contrasts in elevation, humidity and temperature.

All the year round, the hills are steeped in a tangle of blossom and verdure. The valleys, winding down from snowy heights, and carrying streams from the snows to the scorching foothills, are full of vegetation which seldom loses its vivid green. To give a complete account of plant life between, say Siliguri and Darjeeling, or Kangra and Kulu, or Almora and the Pindari Glacier, or Nandprayag and Tungnath, would be well-nigh impossible. One might as well attempt,

To count the leaves of all the trees
To count the waves of all the seas.

One can only touch upon a few representative species and try to convey to the reader an impression of the floral delights that await the trekker, the lover of mountains, and the amateur botanist.

In the lower foothills, the greater number of trees are deciduous. They acclaim the spring with an outburst of blossom. Looking down from the higher land, they appear as a mosaic of colours, each tone denoting a particular species in early flower before heavy leafage is put out.

This variety is very characteristic of tropical vegetation, where propagation depends almost entirely upon the agency of bird, beast or insect, to carry the seed far and wide. Quite different are the tracts of gregarious oak, pine and fir which flourish higher up, fanning out like armies on the move but preferring the company of their own kith and kin.

Amongst the brilliantly coloured giants of the foothills, few trees excel the red silk cotton (*Bombax malabaficum*). Straight as a temple shaft, and clothed in clustering crimson chalices, these trees welcome every creature who, by sipping of the abundant and intoxicating nectar, carries the pollen from flower to flower—thus assisting in the great scheme of species salvation. To add to the beauty and attractiveness of the tree, many bright birds frequent it in search of nectar from the flowers. Mynas, rosy pastors and other small birds keep up a constant chatter. Occasionally the flowers are yellow or white, and the yellow-flowered tree is credited with miraculous powers, human and divine, according to popular belief. For this reason, the tree often suffers at the hands of devotees who wish to possess some of the bark or wood of the tree.

A sheet of scarlet, no less brilliant than that of the silk cotton, proclaims the dhak (*Eiythrina*) in bloom. Orange patches indicate where the sacred palas or flame of the forest (*Butea frondosa*) had found foothold in open and waterlogged spots; pink and white, or purple, where bauhinia reigns supreme, for this tree is an early resident of the foothills of the Himalayas. Cassias of many kinds load themselves with a brilliant gold. The lovely white chalta (*Dillenia indices*) is scattered throughout the forest; and the kadam (*Nauclea cadumba*) hangs out conspicuous golden balls.

The country almonds either show a whole series of brilliant colours in fading leaves, or having changed their dress are subdued in bright green sprays. The dainty verdure of the sisoo (*Dalbergia*), and the tender pink of new-born peepal foliage, fill all the intervening space.

The trees are scaled by a multitude of creepers: many kinds of acacia (*Beaumontia grandiflora*), a mass of snowy trumpets which, when found among the crimsoned chalices of the red cotton, has a wonderfully decorative effect; and the *Bauhinia vahlii* that scarcely puts out a leaf until it attains the level greenery of the treetops. It is like a huge python, winding round and round its victim.

Wightea gigantea sends up a strong stem alongside its prospective victim and keeps an absolutely independent growth at first. It then throws out colossal, horizontal roots, which coalesce and form a fatal network round the trunk. This envelopes and sometimes conceals the tree it embraces, except for the highest branches. These, dry and withered, wave like distress signals far above those of its destroyer. The wood of this creeping monster is used exclusively for the making of images.

Thunbergia grandiflora canopies the tallest trees in wide, lilac flowers, and is a great nectar mart for bees. *Spatholobus roxburghii*, if it refrains from killing its host, will adorn it with long trails of reddish bloom.

The undergrowth in these moist subtropical forests is largely composed of acacias: *Mimosa pudica*, a sensitive and apparently bashful plant, for at the slightest touch the leaflets bend down. Calotropis, on the other hand, might be a fit emblem for boldness, for it flourishes in almost any soil. Called madar in Hindi, it is reputed to be full of good qualities and yields a kind of manna called *madar ka shakkar* (sugar), traditionally used in the treatment of leprosy. And the silky floss is excellent for making pillows! The buds form one of the five flowers on the darts with which Kama-deva, the Hindu god of love, is given to piercing the hearts of mortals.

These forests, particularly in the moist eastern Himalayas, are home to many orchids: *Vanda teres*, muffling its stick-like foliage in beautiful purple flowers; *Arundina*, stiff and precise in form, growing like a reed, but in the early monsoon decorated with large mauve blossoms. *Aerides*, among the most beautiful of orchids with rich evergreen foliage and deliciously scented flowers of a peculiar waxy elegance, are found in the marshy tracts above Siliguri. *Vanda roxburghii* bears spikes of flowers with a chessboard pattern of brown and cream, so singular in its effect that it cannot fail to attract the attention of fertilizing insects.

Ascending the gravelly spurs, the principal tree is sal (*Shorea robusta*). It demands a loose, water-transmitting soil covered with decomposing leaves and other debris of the forest.

Very gregarious, though permitting a few favourites to exist within its regime as 'associates', it covers the subtropical foothills with remarkable celerity. The seeds, ripe for germination, are blown far and wide by the monsoon winds. The rootlets of the young trees are always busily engaged in finding a site of permanent moisture. As soon as this is discovered, up is thrust a sturdy young growth of saplings, each a member of the princely family of palms: *Phoenix humilis*, a dwarf variety rising stemless to yield long leaves which are useful for plaiting into mats or converting into brooms; *Calamus rotang*, used for the cane bridges employed in spanning the roaring torrents of Sikkim; *Colocasia antiquorum*, a giant arum whose fleshly tubers provide a staple article of diet and whose enormous glossy leaves are convenient wayside parasols in sudden showers.

Then there is the instinct with only one idea—to lead in the great race for light! The more vigorous sal trees ascend rapidly. The weaker bide their time, until opportunity offers through the death or destruction of their more powerful brethren. The more successful among them attain a height of hundred to hundred and fifty feet, with a clean stem to the first branch at sixty to eighty feet, and showing a girth of twenty feet. A sal forest has a remarkably individual character. From wee sapling to giant patriarch, each growth ruthlessly waits for the downfall of its neighbour.

Sal is the most important tree of the Himalayan foothills, providing the bulk of railway sleepers in India. The flowers, minute and sweet-scented, appear in March, in great panicles accompanying the new leaves. In some places they herald in a spring carnival when baskets of them are borne from village to village and distributed to the women as emblems of motherhood. Buddhists especially revere the sal, since it was beneath a sal tree that the great Teacher died.

Observing Ananda weeping, Gautama said, 'Do not weep, Ananda. This body of ours contains within itself the powers which renew its strength for a time, but also the causes which lead to its destruction. Is there anything put together which shall not dissolve? That which causes life causes also decay and death ...'

These were the last words of Gautama Buddha, as he stretched himself out to die under the great sal tree at Kasinagar.

The sal, though acquisitive of territory, has many associates of arboreal or herbal growth in its vicinity. One such satellite is *Cyeas revotula*, a palm-like structure bearing a crown of rigid leaves and flowers in large, evil-smelling cones. And there are many *Lagerstroemia*, with immense, starry white heads of bloom, over which bees and butterflies throng from dawn to dusk, and in whose dark recesses of shiny leaves the tailorbird sews her nest.

We find the *Loranthus longiflorus*, a heavy parasite with handsome orange flowers, killing all branches to which it attaches itself. And, as if to offset it, the life-reviving *Vitis latifoloa*, whose soft porous stems yield when cut, a quantity of good potable water, is a real boon to those who have to work in these dry and often waterless forests.

Beyond the sal forests the countryside changes in appearance. The undergrowth is not so high. It thins out, often breaking altogether into yellow sheets of mustard. In fact, the only features suggesting tropical vegetation are giant mops of *Pandanus furcatus* popularly known as the screw pine; *Caryota urens*, a palm; and beautiful arborescent ferns.

The prevailing tree fern is *Hemitelia*, rearing itself with the aspect of a palm on a rough, slender stem and crested with a crown of feathery foliage. It can claim extreme antiquity, for its fossil remains were found in coal beds, showing that it once constituted those dense antediluvian forests where a multitude of plants, which are now humble shrubs or weeds, reigned as giants of their kind.

Where there is not a great show of flowering trees, the michelias, near relations of the magnolias, attract notice. Approaching Guptkashi, in Garhwal, my attention was caught by three giant michelias growing beside an abandoned temple a little distance above the banks of the Mandakini river. Why a Shiv temple has been abandoned in this region of intense Hindu pilgrimage was a mystery to me. It was no longer on the main pilgrim route, and that may have accounted for its neglect. But the trees were flourishing, their sweet-scented blossoms strewing the ground and resting against the many lingams that surrounded the shrine.

These tall michelias have dark green, shining leaves and very fragrant flowers which are used as votive offerings at temples. Another species, *Schizandra grandiflora*, also called champa locally, is a climbing shrub with drooping white flowers which lengthen in fruit into a fleshly axis. The michelia is among the first true flowering plants to appear in the geological record. It once knew a very wide geographical distribution, but in the battle for survival it has been worsted and is now confined only to the Himalayas and parts of America.

Birch trees are found in the northwest Himalayas. The birch, *tagpa*, of the Chenab river, is usually a crooked and stunted tree, but sometimes exceeds one foot in diameter. The annual bridges over the mountain torrents are made of birch branches. The thin white bark of the *Betula birch*—bhojpatra— occurs in sheets or pieces, which can be peeled off. It was used for making umbrellas, and is still used for writing on, in lieu of paper. It makes an imperishable thatch when covered with sods of earth. And I have even seen it being used for lining a hookah.

The prevalent poplar is so called by courtesy only. Its broad, heart-shaped, delicately hung leaves, readily fluttering to every breeze, bear a superficial resemblance to members of the poplar family; but in reality it belongs to the witch-hazel family. It is an attractive ornamental tree, popular with those attempting to restore some greenery to the bare slopes of our hill stations. It is not a gregarious forest tree, and is probably best suited to roadside plantation.

In the eastern Himalayas the atmosphere and soil are too humid for some members of the Coniferous family, but they admirably suit the immigrant

Clyptomaria, a cedar introduced around 1920 from Japan. Trim, beautiful and straight it is frequently found between four and six thousand feet. It grows quickly and has the power to withstand all kinds of weather. In Japan it is also grown in hedges and is known as *sugi*.

At an elevation of four to seven thousand feet all the herbal flora of temperate Europe is found: violets, buttercups, cowslips, barberry, primrose, St John's wort, dandelion, stonecrop, periwinkle, commelina, meadow sage, wood sorrel, blackberry, dog rose, sorrel, balsam, poppies, anemones, wild carrot, clover, nettles, wild geranium, nightshade, saxifrage, and alpine rock cress, to list only a few of the many hundreds of wildflowers found at these altitudes from Kashmir in the west to Arunachal Pradesh in the east.

I will describe a few personal favourites.

Perhaps it is the commelina, more than any other flower, that takes one's breath away. Its colour does this; a pure pristine blue that reflects the deepest blue of the sky. Towards the end of the rains it appears as if from nowhere, gladdens the hillside for the space of about two weeks, and then disappears again until the following monsoon. I stand dumb before it; and the world stands still while I worship. It makes me doubt the reality of everything in the world. In Europe it is a charming garden flower, but in its home in the temperate Himalayas it seems to resist any attempt at domestication, growing almost anywhere except in captivity.

Several varieties of balsam, or *Impatients*, flourish between seven and nine thousand feet. The term *impatients* refers to the hasty escape of the seed when the pod is touched. When fully ripe, the pod explodes at the slightest touch. Frank Smythe, in his *Valley of Flowers* (1930), describes masses of balsam growing as tall as eight feet in the Bhyunder valley and adjoining areas of the Garhwal Himalayas.

The anemone and alpine rock cress grow on the steep meadows below Tungnath (eleven thousand feet) in Garhwal, and buttercups and wild strawberries are to be found throughout Kumaon, Garhwal, Himachal, wherever it is cool and moist.

On the bare southern slopes of the hill station of Mussoorie, where little seems to grow, a pink crocus (called by some a thunder lily) pops up in the soil at the first summer shower, flowers brilliantly for a few days, and then subsides, leaving no clue to its whereabouts. In this way it has survived.

In Kashmir the crocus is cultivated for its saffron. This is the saffron crocus, *Crocus sativus*, an autumn-flowering plant, the flowers violet with long tubes, sweet-scented. The dried stigmas of this crocus constitute the genuine saffron of commerce.

Various species of primula and saxifrage are found throughout the Himalayas, while the prevalence of the rambling dog rose reminds us that it is the forerunner of the beautiful hybrid blooms now cultivated throughout the world. In May, the hills around Chakrata are bestowed with dog roses and masses of wild daisies.

Wild yellow roses are found in Kashmir, Lahaul and Tibet. Early travellers mention double yellow roses at eleven thousand feet in Ladakh. Phulian, or ban-gulab (*Rosa macrophylla*), the great red rose tree, grows over a wide range in the northwestern Himalayas, from four thousand five hundred to ten thousand five hundred feet. Its fruit is eaten, becoming very sweet when black and rotten. It is one of the most beautiful of the Himalayan plants, though not as common as it used to be; its flowers are as large as the palm of the hand.

Rosa sericea is an erect, white-flowered rose, the only species occurring in southern Sikkim. It is quite abundant, its numerous flowers pendent, apparently as a protection from the rain; and it is remarkable as being the only species having four petals instead of five.

Rosa webbiana (kugina) is found chiefly in the arid tracts of the Himalayas from five to nine thousand feet, up to the near Indus, and in Ladakh it is known to reach thirteen thousand five hundred feet. Its fruit is eaten, and in parts of Spiti the stems are used for fuel.

Edible berries, such as the barbery (kingora in Garhwal) and raspberry (hissa), are great favourites with the hill children, who have to walk many miles from home to school and back again, and often restore their flagging energies with whatever wild fruit is in season. The rhododendron petals are also edible, and make a good jam or chutney.

In the hills of Garhwal I have sometimes found a tiny blue and white iris growing here and there in the stony soil. It is the kind botanists call *pumila*, the little one. It is a reminder of the great range of forms and sizes, habits and habitats of this fascinating family which has something like two hundred wild species scattered around the northern Hemisphere.

A broad-leaved species of iris grows throughout the western Himalayas from two thousand five hundred to nine thousand five hundred feet. The beautiful fugitive flowers of the Kashmir iris, a distinct species, luxuriates over every grave, and blooms on many a housetop (growing out of the earth-daubed roofs) in the valley—a custom resembling that of the ancient Greeks, who venerated the iris as the messenger between God and man.

Remember, too, that the iris is a flower of innumerable tints, and as the hues of the rainbow are seen by the human eye, so the eye, which is the sole source of our knowledge of colour, is the symbol of the iris.

The wild cinnamon is common throughout the hills. The young shoots of the tree are often a dark crimson, a provision of nature for the absorption of

the solar rays so that the life-giving green granules
of the leaf may be preserved until a leathery protective
epidermis is formed. The flowers are incomplete, as
there are no petals. The bark and leaves are full of
an aromatic oil which is well known in commerce.

Begonias are found in all the shady dells. The
great yellow flower, begonia, is abundant in the
Bablang pass in the Sikkim Himalayas. Its juicy
stalks are used to make sauce, the taste is acid and
very pleasant. The remarkable variegation of their
large one-sided leaves has made them favourite
foliage plants.

Magnificent orchids grow in profusion on rocks
or decorate moss-grown branches with their fragile
loveliness. Some shake out a golden spray; some
wave delicate lilac and lemon panicles in the breeze;
some show golden cones. Strange *Cirrhopetalums*
hold little brown wings over their backs or form a
flower one inch in length trailing appendages two to
three feet long. Spider-like *Arachnanthe* opens a
flower of yellow so evenly striped with transverse
bands of brown that it has earned for itself the local
name of bagh-chanira (leopard flower).

Delicate *Cynibidiums* fasten themselves to
branches with thick, spongy roots and trail long
sprays of elegant flowers, some very fragrant, others
positively unpleasant.

Cypripediums (orchids of the ladies slipper
species), fairly widespread in the Himalayas, both

east and west, swing up a flaunting beauty from the ground in which they lie concealed until the monsoon rains bring them to life. Then, in green, purple, or white arrangements, they display the slipper-like development of one of the petals—one of the most cunning blandishments in Nature's workshop for securing the assistance of insects in fertilization.

These orchids—of which there are over forty species—sometimes follow mountain chains on which they occur in small groups or are isolated at great distances from each other. In other instances they are confined to islands or groups of islands, growing chiefly on ledges or in positions where there is a small accumulation of decayed vegetable matter. Sometimes they are exposed to the sun's rays, but more frequently they are found under the shelter of overhanging trees.

Many rare orchids in the eastern Himalayas are in the process of extinction—yielding ground, along with other fugitive flora, to the pressures of population and cultivation. Illegal exports have also taken their toll.

Higher up, the character of the forest changes. The trees are more massive and sombre-looking, and in the moister regions they carry heavy epiphytal burdens: mosses hanging in queer fantastic shapes; orchids; *Usnea barbata*, the old man's beard; lichen hanging like bunches of hoary hair; and a host of other parasitic giants so aptly called banda (slaves) by the hill folk.

Sometimes, though, these hangers-on are not content with the support afforded to them, and actually prey on their hosts, causing considerable damage. This is particularly so in the case of *Viscum* and *Loranthus* of the mistletoe family, which kill the branches beyond the places of their attachment, by insinuating their slender rootlets through the interstices right down to the sapwood. Here they form suckers by means of which they completely drain the branch. Even the lichens, although quite harmless in themselves, afford resting places for the seeds of other plants on the lookout for hospitality.

From five to nine thousand feet, there are several varieties of oak: *Quercus lamellosa*, the bak, attains a height of hundred feet and after a century of growth becomes hollow though it has a girth of twenty to thirty feet. Its acorns are large, two to three inches in diameter. This oak comprises most of the Himachal forest.

Q. pachyphylla (barakatus) also has very large acorns, occuring in threes and bedded deeply in their scaly cups. *Q. Spicata* does not ascend beyond five thousand feet and carries its acorns on spikes. *Q. acuminata* is the species found on Birch Hill, Darjeeling; the leaves are silvery beneath. These are all oaks of the eastern Himalayas. Above nine thousand feet in Sikkim, they are replaced by a species of hazel (Corylus).

In the northwestern Himalayas, on the other hand, the common hoary oak or karsu is amongst the most alpine of trees growing up to eleven thousand feet. This is *Q. semecarpifolia*. Other oaks, found throughout Himachal, Garhwal and Kumaon, are the ban or banj (*Q. incana*) and moru (*Q. dilatata*), which is next in importance to the pines. Vast forests of them occur in various places, and the trees—if not lopped—attain a great size, eighty to hundred feet in height. They prefer dry situations, and are not generally found close to a river.

Of the Conifers, *Pinus longifola* (chil or thanea) is the most common, growing from three to seven thousand feet, from Simla to Darjeeling and Kangra to Bhutan. It endures the most heat and the greatest variation in the amount of moisture. This is the pine from which we get our resin and turpentine.

Pinus excelsa (chir) is also found extensively in Garhwal, Simla, Sirmour, Bhutan and Nepal, but at higher altitude, ranging from seven to eleven thousand feet. You can recognize it from its drooping branches. It also grows sparingly in western Tibet.

Pinus Gerardians (chilgoza, neoza) is confined to the northern and drier slopes of the Himalayas. Above Chini (on the Hindustan-Tibet road) it is the principal tree of the forest, producing a very large cone containing edible nuts which, when roasted like chestnuts, are agreeable to taste, though with a slight flavour of turpentine. The seeds, of which there are more than a hundred in a cone, are collected and stored for winter use, being a regular article of food in Tibet and Afghanistan.

The deodar (*Cedrus deodarus*, Himalayan cedar) gets its name from the Sanskrit deva-daru (divine tree), and this is its name in Garhwal and Kumaon; but in the Jaunsar Bawar district of Garhwal and in Himachal it is known as the kelu or kelon. Its timber is always used in temples for doors, walls and roofs.

No one would deny that the deodar is the noblest and most godlike of all Himalayan trees. It stands erect, and though in a strong wind it may hum and moan, it does not bend to the wind. The snow slips softly off its resilient branches. It thrives in the rain and it likes the company of its own kind, preferring the sheltered moisture-laden mountain sides to those facing the prevailing winds.

The average girth of the larger deodars is about fifteen to twenty feet, but isolated trees often attain a greater size. One giant deodar (measured by Madden in the last century) was two hundred and fifty feet high, twenty feet in girth at the base, and more than five hundred and fifty years old. Such giants are rare today, most of them having fallen to the axe in the 1950s, a decade when India, and in particular the Indian Himalayas, suffered greatly from deforestation.

The timber of the deodar has always been highly prized for house building (especially in Jaunsar Bawar and parts of Himachal, where deodars are most at home), and for building boats, railway sleepers and bridges. The timber is not affected by extremes of climate. The pillars of the great mosque built by Aurangzeb at Srinagar (Kashmir) show no signs of decay, although exposed to the action of water for over four hundred years. Many deodar bridges in Srinagar, along the Jhelum, are even older.

Perhaps my favourite Himalayan tree is the horse chestnut; extremely friendly and cheerful, especially when in full foliage. It is bare in winter, allowing the sun to stream through its straight, smooth branches. In March, the leaf-buds appear. In April, the blossoms, pale pink candelabra, hang in clusters, attracting bees and small birds. In May and June, when the sun is really hot even in these higher altitudes, the tree is in full leaf, providing welcome shade. The leaves rustle in the slightest breeze, chattering and gossiping among themselves for hours on end. Towards the end of the rains the chestnuts ripen, providing endless enjoyment for small boys, who play with them, and for long-tailed langurs, who feed on them. Then the leaves fall, curling slowly downwards until they form a crumbling yellow carpet on the hillside.

There are other chestnuts. *C. trifuloides* has

velvety young leaves which later become firm and shining; the fruit is loved by Lepchas, and the wood provides the big pestles and mortars used for crushing the grain of a millet which is converted into the local beer. *C. argentea* is a lofty tree with edible nuts.

In the more exposed places grew the maples, trees of no great size or thickness but easily distinguished even at a distance, especially in the 'sunset of the year' when their foliage reveals an astonishing variety of crimson and gold tints. They can also be recognized by their peculiar reddish brown fruit and distinctive leaves. *A. hookerii* is the most frequent at seven thousand feet. *A. sikkimensis* has its young leaves bright green and serrate, which become entire and heart-shaped as they grow older. *A. oblongum* with oblong leaves, green above, whitish and hairy below is a moderate-sized tree with a wood close-grained and elastic; the best drinking cups in Tibet are made from the knobs of this tree.

Juglans regia, the walnut, is a native of the Himalayas. *Juglans* means the nuts of Jove, for in the Golden Age, they were preserved as food for the Gods, man being content to live on acorns! In Germany, at one time, it was compulsory for a young man to plant a certain number of walnut trees before he could marry.

A bit of folklore common to both East and West is that the walnut is good for the brain, this belief arising from the fact that the fruit of the walnut is shaped almost exactly like the human brain.

On the Hindustan-Tibet road, a wonderful trek when I was a boy, walnuts grew in abundance in the wide Chini valley. In the month of August the whole valley was golden with ripe apricots and in the same season the vineyards near the river produced luscious grapes of many varieties. The climate was well suited to fruit growing. Peaches, pears, plums, apricots, apples, all grew in profusion, along with many kinds of garden produce. In the forest bungalow at Pangi was a large table of deodar wood almost completely covered with the self-carved names of travellers who had passed that way. The oldest names were those of two officers of the fourth Hussars, inscribed September 1870.

Ramgarh, in Kumaon, was the place to be in apple-blossom time. One was literally hemmed in on all sides by a riot of white, a sea of apple blossoms.

Apples were first introduced in the Himalayan valleys by European settlers who started the first big orchards: Wilson at Harsil (near Gangotri), Banon in Kulu, and Wheeler in Ramgarh. The lower end of the Ramgarh valley is five thousand and five hundred feet above sea level against the upper end's seven thousand and five hundred feet, enabling about two hundred varieties of apple to grow, as well as peaches, cherries and apricots.

The visitor to Ramgarh should proceed further

and savour the delights of a trek to the Pindari
Glacier. The great tree rhododendron accompanies
you most of the way, as well as walnuts, chestnuts
and oaks. Dutch clover, honeysuckle, wild thyme,
blue sage and larkspur tempt you to stop again and
again. But perhaps most memorable of all (in spring)
are the blue primroses that at Dhakuri and Dwali
thrust their heads up through the snow.

The rhododendron is probably the most admired
tree throughout the Himalayas. Its magnificent
clusters of pink or crimson bells explain the derivation
of the generic name, *rhodon* (rose), *dendron* (tree),
rose tree.

In Sikkim, in the last century, Dr Hooker
gathered, in two days, seeds of twenty-four kinds of
rhododendrons. In the delicacy and beauty of their
flowers, four of them stand out; they are
Rh. aucklandi whose flowers are five and half inches
in diameter; *Rh. maddeni*, *Rh. dalhousie* and
Rh. edgworthii, all white-flowered bushes of which
the first two rise to the height of small trees.

In the Tonglo mountains, in Sikkim, the trees in
order of prevalence were the scarlet *Rh. arborcum*
and *barbatum*, the latter thirty to forty feet high,
both loaded with beautiful flowers and luxuriant
foliage; and *Rh. falconeri*, from the point of foliage
the most superb of all the Himalayan species.

Rh. arboreum (the bras of Kumaon and Garhwal,
the urvail of Jhelum, and 'mandal' of Himachal) is

the tree rhododendron, growing at an altitude of eight thousand feet in the northwestern Himalayas. It is one of the most beautiful of all trees, having a gnarled trunk and deep crimson flowers in masses. The bright red, slightly acidic flowers, are made into jelly. The soft brown wood was once used for making charcoal and for building houses of the zamindars.

Rh.argenteum, the white-flowered rhododendron, is found in Sikkim at an elevation of eight thousand and six hundred feet. Its leaves are very beautiful, the leaf-buds erect and silky. It outlives the scarlet rhododendron and grows as tall as forty feet, with magnificent leaves twelve to fifteen inches long, deep green, wrinkled above and silvery below. Few plants exceed in beauty the flowering branch of this tree with its wide-spreading foliage and glorious mass of flowers.

Another beautiful Himalayan species is *Rh. barbatum*, a tree forty to sixty feet high, branched from the base.

Rh. campanulatum is found in the Sutlej valley between Rampur and Sungnam, at an elevation of ten to fourteen thousand feet, and on the Kashmir mountains. The leaves from the Tibetan and Kashmiri varieties glory in the names of *Barg-i-Tibet* and *Hulas-i-Kashmiri*, and are used as snuff. They produce vigorous sneezing. The tree is quite abundant and the bark is used for paper-making.

Rhododendron cinnabarinum (the kema kechoong of the Lepchas) is, on the other hand, to be avoided. It is said to be poisonous, and when used as fuel causes the face to swell and the eyes to inflame.

Rh. falconeri, a white-flowered species, never occuring at less then ten thousand feet, is one of the most striking and distinct of the genus. It is found in eastern Nepal, and from the point of foliage is perhaps the most superb of all the Himalayan species, with trunks forty feet high and leaves nineteen inches long. The leaves are deep green above, and covered beneath with a rich brown down.

Rh. nivale spreads its small rigid branches close to the ground. The most alpine of woody plants, it was found by Dr Hooker at an elevation of seventeen thousand and five hundred feet. There are a number of other varieties, and we must not forget to mention *Rh. wallichii*, with its lilac-coloured flowers.

Associated with the rhododendrons are the magnolias, of which there are three varieties; *Magnolia excelsa*, the prevailing white-flowered one, which blossoms so profusely in April that parts of the hillside appear to be snowed over; *M. cambelii* is more sparingly branched, but has immense pink cups which unfortunately fall early; and a deep wine-coloured magnolia (very similar to that found in Japan), which is perhaps the most handsome as it is the most fragrant—behaving quite against the

Darwinian theory that white flowers smell sweeter than red.

Magnolias have been known to produce nausea by the strength of their sweetness, so that 'to die of a rose in aromatic pain' is not so great a flight of poetic imagination as might be thought.

Michelia lanuginosa is found at six thousand feet with white flowers and long velvety leaves. America is said to be the home of the species, but the Sikkim Himalayas show many more varieties than do the Rocky Mountains, and they are far more gorgeous. At one time these exquisite trees were exported widely to the world's gardens, thriving in northern Europe where they adapted well to the rigorous climate.

Of the bamboo, the most gigantic of the grasses, there are many genera and species, varying greatly in size. Many beautiful bamboos abound in the hills: some converted into the drinking vessels of the Lepchas; some used in floating heavy logs; and others in roofing, for which purpose the columns are cut short and flattened out, to serve as tiles; they are considered durable and absolutely watertight.

The town of Dehra Dun, about hundred and fifty years ago, was chiefly noted for its clusters and avenues of large bamboos, 'forming the principal feature in the beauty of the Doon ever since the valley became known to us' (Capt. Sleeman). They must have died out, or been cut down to make way for buildings in an ever-expanding city; today there are only a few corners where these great bamboos can still be seen.

In September, towards the end of the rains, the hillside is covered with a sward of flowers and ferns: sprays of wild ginger, tangles of clematis, flat clusters of yarrow and lady's mantle. *Dastura stramonium* grows everywhere with its graceful white bells and prickly fruits. And the wild woodbine, *Lonicera formosa*, provides flutes for the hill boys.

Aroids of the genus *Arisoema* are quite plentiful throughout the Himalayas, and attract attention by the extraordinary resemblance to a snake with a protruding tongue—hence their popular name, cobra lily.

As a family they cannot lay claim either to beauty or fragrance, though so nearly related to the lovely Nile lily. Their abominable scent is, however, one of Nature's marvellous provisions for fertilization, since flies and beetles and other noxious creatures distribute their pollen. If the spathe is opened, the central stem will be seen to be covered with minute petal-less florets arranged in rings, sometimes each sex on a separate spike; at other times both in one house but with the males in a higher belt. The serpent's tongue is an admirable landing-stage for flies, etc. who, crawling over the male flowers in their eager search for the liquor that lies at the base of the spike and is most appealing to their depraved appetites, fertilize the female flowers as they proceed.

Arisoema wallichii, a plant with a handsome black and white mottled stalk and a heavy crown of three large leaves, bears its deep purple spathe close to the ground, for the convenience of its special visitors—the ants and other crawling insects.

A. helleborifolium is much more elegant, having a crown of slender leaflets and a delicate green spathe ribbed with white, and the spadix prolongs into a far-protruding thread. This is the first of the aroids to appear, even before the rains commence.

Another cobra lily, which rejoices in the name of *Sauromatum guttatum*, bears a solitary leaf and purple spathe. When the seeds form, it withdraws the spike underground, and when the rains are over and the soil is less moist, sends it up covered with scarlet berries. In the opinion of the hill people the appearance of the red spike is more to be relied on as a forecast of the end of the monsoon rains than any meteorological expertise. Up here in the temperate Himalayas we can be perfectly sure of fine weather a fortnight after that fiery spike appears.

V

Trees

Trees have always played an important part in my life. The litchi, guava, mango, jackfruit and lemon trees of my childhood. Later, the grandeur of the banyan, the sacred peepal, the sal and the shisham. And here in the hills, the stately deodars and fragrant pines. Long ago, I made some notes, short essays, on some favourite trees, and now I share these with my readers.

The Guardians of My Conscience

The trees stand watch over my day-to-day life. They are the guardians of my conscience. I have no one else to answer to, so I live and work under the generous but highly principled supervision of the trees—especially the deodars, who stand on guard, unbending, on the slope above the cottage. The oak and maples are a little more tolerant, they have had to put up with a great deal, their branches continually lopped for fuel and fodder. 'What would they think?' I ask myself on many an occasion. 'What would they like me to do?' And I do what I think they would approve of most!

Well, it's nice to have someone to turn to ...

The leaves are a fresh pale green in the spring rain. I can look at the trees from my window—look down on them almost, because the window is on the first floor of the cottage, and the hillside runs at a sharp angle into the ravine. I do nearly all my writing at this window seat. Whenever I look up, the trees remind me that they are there. They are my best critics. As long as I am aware of their presence, I can try to avoid the trivial and the banal.

Notes on My Favourite Trees

Dehra was a good place for trees, and Grandfather's house was surrounded by several kinds—peepal, neem, mango, jackfruit, papaya and the ancient banyan. Some of them were planted by Grandfather and grew up with me.

There were two kinds of trees that were of special interest to me—trees that were good for climbing, and trees that provided fruit.

The jackfruit tree had both these qualities. The fruit itself—the largest in the world—grew only on the trunk and main branches. It was not my favourite fruit, and I preferred it cooked as a vegetable. But the tree was large and leafy and easy to climb.

The peepal was a good tree to sit beneath on hot days. Its heart-shaped leaves, sensitive to the slightest breeze, would flip gently when the clouds stood still and not another tree witnessed the least movement in the air. There is a peepul tree in every Indian village, and it is common to see a farmer, tired at the end of an afternoon's toil in the fields, being lulled to sleep by the rustling of its leaves.

A banyan tree, as old as the town of Dehra itself, grew behind our house. Its spreading branches, which hung to the ground and took root again, formed a number of twisting passageways which gave me endless pleasure. I could hide myself in its branches, behind thick green leaves, and spy on the world below. I could read in it too, propped up against the bole of the tree with my favourite books.

The banyan tree was a world in itself, populated with small beasts and large insects. While the leaves were still pink and tender, they would be visited by the delicate map butterfly, who committed her eggs to their care. The 'honey' on the leaves—an edible smear—also attracted the little striped squirrels, who soon grew used to my presence in the tree and became quite bold, accepting peanuts from my hand. Red-headed parakeets swarmed about early in the mornings.

At the height of the monsoon, the banyan was like an orchestra-pit with the musicians constantly tuning up. Birds, insects and squirrels expressed their joy at the termination of the hot weather and the cool quenching relief of the monsoon. A toy flute in my hands, I would try adding my shrill piping to theirs. But they thought poorly of my musical ability, for, whenever I piped, the birds and the insects maintained a pained and puzzled silence.

The branches were thick with scarlet figs. These berries were not fit for human consumption, but the many birds that gathered in the tree—gossipy rosy pastors, quarrelsome mynas, cheerful bulbuls and coppersmiths, and sometimes a raucous, bullying crow—feasted on them. And when night fell, and the birds rested, the dark flying foxes flapped heavily about the tree, chewing and munching as they clambered over the branches.

One of my favourite trees in Dehra was the jamun, also known as the Java plum. Its purple astringent fruit ripened during the rains, and then I would join the gardener's young son in its branches, and we would feast like birds on the smooth succulent fruit until our lips and cheeks were stained a bright purple.

After I moved to Mussoorie in my thirties, I lived for many years in a cottage at seven thousand feet in the Garhwal Himalayas. I was fortunate in having a big window that opened out on the forest, so that the trees were almost within my reach. Had I jumped, I should have landed safely in the arms of an oak or chestnut.

The incline of the hill was such that my first-floor window opened on what must, I suppose, have been the second floor. I never made the jump, but the big silver-red langurs, with long swishing tails, often leapt from the trees onto the corrugated tin roof and made enough noise to disturb the bats sleeping in the space between the roof and ceiling.

Standing on its own was a walnut tree, and truly, this was a tree for all seasons. In winter its branches were bare, and smooth and straight and round like the arms of a woman in a painting by Jamini Roy. In spring each branch produced a hard bright spear of new leaves. By mid-summer the entire tree was in leaf, and towards the end of the monsoon the walnuts, encased in their green jackets, had reached maturity. Then the jackets began to split, revealing the hard black shell of the walnuts. Inside the shell was the nut itself, shaped rather like the human brain. (No wonder the ancients prescribed walnuts for headaches!)

I went among the trees on my hillside often, acknowledging their presence with a touch of my hand against their trunks—the walnut's smooth and polished; the pine's patterned and whorled; the oak's rough and gnarled, full of experience. The oak had been there the longest, and the wind had bent its upper branches and twisted a few, so that it looked shaggy and undistinguished. It was a good tree for the privacy of birds, its crooked branches spreading out with no particular effect; and sometimes the tree seemed uninhabited until there was a whirring sound, as of a helicopter approaching, and a party of long-tailed blue magpies shot out of the tree and streamed across the forest glade.

After the monsoon, when the dark red berries had ripened on the hawthorn, this pretty tree was visited by green pigeons, the kokla birds of Garhwal, who clambered upside-down among the fruit-laden twigs. And during winter, a white-capped redstart perched on the bare branches of the wild pear tree and whistled cheerfully. He had come to winter in the garden.

The pines grew on the next hill—the chir, the Himalayan blue pine, and the long-leaved pine—but there was a small blue one a little way below my cottage, and sometimes I sat beneath it to listen to the wind playing softly in its branches.

Opening the window at night, I usually had something to listen to, the mellow whistle of the pygmy owlet, or the cry of a barking deer which had scented the proximity of a panther.

Some sounds I could not recognize at the time. They were strange night sounds that I now know as the sounds of the trees themselves, scratching their limbs in the dark, shifting a little, flexing their fingers. Great trees of the mountains, they know me well. They know my face in the window, they see me watching them, watching them grow, listening to their secrets, bowing my head before their outstretched arms and seeking their benediction.

Sometimes, there would be a strange silence, and I would see the moon coming up, and two distant deodars in perfect silhouette.

No tree lover, even if he or she is a city dweller, can ignore the sal and the mahua, two of the most splendid and most valuable of our trees.

The sal can be grown in a city, but it does not

like being alone; it is much happier amongst its own kind in the forests that cover the moist foothills and plateau lands of northern and central India. It is a valuable timber tree, and in northern India most of the wood used in buildings comes from the sal. But it is not only the wood that is useful. When tapped, the sal yields a large quantity of resin, which is burnt as incense in Hindu religious ceremonies. The resin is also used to caulk boats and ships. The large, shiny leaf is sometimes put to good use too. The Santals of Bihar gather fresh sal leaves daily, and use them as plates or as drinking cups. When fitted cleverly into one another, the leaves make excellent plates for holding dal and rice, while one large sal leaf, twisted round to form a hollow, will hold water quite effectively.

The leaf is used for building too: not by men, but by ants! The nest of the red ant consists of a mass of green or dead sal leaves stuck together with a sort of gum which the adult ant extracts from the young ant grubs. If you examine one of these nests (do not disturb it!) you will find it humming with ant life. But do not try making pets of these ants; they are as aggressive as the big bees, and bite quite fiercely, as many a shikari has known to his discomfort when he has brushed against a nest when out hunting on an elephant.

Another insect inhabiting the sal tree is the cicada. You may have heard it singing away through the long hot weather and the rains. One cicada is shrill enough; a forest full of singing cicadas is like an orchestra tuning up, each musician trying out a different tune. Even the birds are shocked into silence.

The sal takes the place of the peepal among the tribes of central India, and when the tree blossoms in March a festival called the Bahbonga is held. During marriages, two poles, one of bamboo, the other of sal wood, are set up in the marriage-shed, and these are anointed with oil and turmeric. If one of the couple is unwilling to go through with the marriage, he or she may take a leaf of the sal and tear it in two.

There is a tradition that at the time of the Buddha's birth, his mother stretched out her hand to hold a branch of a sal tree, and was delivered of her child. Sal trees are also said to have rendered homage to the Buddha at his death by letting their flowers fall on him out of season, and bending their branches to shade him.

The beautiful mahua is another forest tree that plays an important part in the lives of the tribal people. The flowers of the mahua can be eaten, raw or cooked, and are an important item of the food of the Gonds and other tribes in central and western India, particularly in time of drought when rice is scarce. In fact, the poorer people depend almost entirely upon the mahua crop.

From the seeds of the mahua, an oil is extracted which can be used for lighting as well as for cooking (as a substitute for ghee). Oil from the seeds is also used in the manufacture of soap.

The mahua tree bursts into full bloom at the very beginning of the hot weather, when the fortunes of the tribal people are usually rather low. As it is the slack season among cultivators, the gathering of the mahua blossoms is a welcome task, the whole village often turning out to bring in the crop. Sometimes the grass under the mahua tree is burnt so that the blossoms may be gathered more easily. The women equip themselves with baskets, piling them one on top of the other on their heads, and the children carry brooms so that after all the blossoms have been gathered the ground can be cleared in readiness for the next fall.

During the short period—only about fifteen days—that the mahua blossoms fall, the villagers practically live in the jungle, the men carrying away the crop as fast as the women and children can collect it.

Laid out to dry on a smooth bare patch of ground that has been especially cleared and prepared, the blossoms become quite dry and shrink to half their normal size, changing from white to brown. The mahua is often eaten by itself, but sometimes sal seeds and rice are mixed with it to improve the flavour. The mahua is first boiled; the sal seeds, which have already been dried in the sun and roasted, are then added with a small quantity of rice.

Wild animals, particularly bears, are fond of the flowers of the mahua, but no one, human or animal, has to climb the tree to gather them. The tree blooms at night, and the flowers fall to the ground at dawn.

The Gentle Banyan

Just as tall men are often the most gentle, so are big trees the most friendly. The banyan is probably the biggest and friendliest of all our trees.

We don't see many banyan trees in our cities nowadays. These trees like to have plenty of space in which to spread themselves out, but in our overcrowded cities, where there is barely enough living space for people, banyan trees don't have much of a chance. After all, a full-grown banyan takes up as large an area as a three-storeyed apartment building! Of course, many parks have banyan trees. And every village has at least one.

The banyan has, what are called, 'aerial roots', that is, its branches drop to the ground, take root again, and send out more twisting, trailing branches, so that after some years the tree forms a forest glade of its own. No wonder, the banyan was chosen to represent the matted hair of Shiva!

The aerial roots of the banyan are like pillars supporting a great palace. If you destroy the pillars, the palace will fall, and so will the banyan, because its main trunk isn't very deeply rooted. So naturally it needs plenty of space in which to put out its supporting roots. Tiny gardens and busy roadsides won't do. Nor should the tree be planted too close to your house: you might find it growing through your bedroom wall!

It is always cool, dark and shady beneath the banyan. And it is a good tree for climbing. You can get up amongst its branches without much difficulty, and there is no danger of falling off. It is also one of the most comfortable trees to sit in. You can lean against its broad trunk and read a book, without any fear of being disturbed, for you will be completely hidden by the broad, glossy leaves.

The banyan is also very hospitable. Apart from boys and girls, it attracts a large number of visitors—birds, squirrels, insects, flying foxes—and many of these interesting creatures actually live in the tree which is full of dark, private corners suitable for a variety of tenants. The banyan is rather like a hotel or boarding house in which a number of different families live next door to each other without interfering very much in each other's business.

The banyan belongs to the fig family, and, in

India all the figs—the best known of which is the peepal—are held sacred. The Akshaya Vata, the 'undying' banyan tree at the sacred confluence of the rivers at Allahabad, is the subject of many legends, and still attracts millions of pilgrims. It was first described by Huen Tsang, the Chinese pilgrim, who visited India over a thousand years ago.

A group of three sacred trees known as tentar, 'triad'—a banyan, a peepal and a paakar planted together—is especially sacred, and is known as Harsankari, 'the chair of Hari (Shiva)'.

In Hindi the banyan is known as the bar, in Tamil, the ala. But how did it get its English name? Well, it seems that the first Europeans who came to India noticed that the tree was a favourite with the banias, the Hindu merchant class, who used to gather beneath it for worship or business. So they gave it the name banian, which later became banyan.

Lest you should feel that the banyan is a magnificent giant of little or no value to man, it should be remembered that its wood, which is tough and elastic, has for centuries been used for making tent poles and yokes for bullock-carts, while its leaves and twigs have always been a favourite snack with the elephants.

Avenues of banyan trees are not as common as they used to be, and roadside banyans can often be seen with their beautiful supporting roots cut off—a sad spectacle. No other tree provides so much cool, refreshing shade on a hot summer's day, and for this reason, if for no other, this noble tree deserves our love and care.

These lines by George Morris could well be applied to the friendly banyan:

Woodman, spare that tree!
Touch not a single bough!
In youth it sheltered me,
And I'll protect it now.

The Tree of Wisdom

In some ways peepal trees are great show-offs. Even when there is no breeze, their beautiful leaves spin like tops, determined to attract your attention and invite you into their shade. And not only do they send down currents of cool air, but their long slender tips are also constantly striking together to make a sound like the pattering of raindrops.

No wonder the rishis of old chose to sit and meditate under these trees. And it was beneath a peepal that, Gautama Buddha gained enlightenment. This tree came to be called the Bodhi, the 'tree of wisdom'.

To the Hindus, the peepal is especially sacred. Its roots, it is believed, represent Brahma, its bark

Vishnu, its branches Shiva. 'As the wide-spreading peepal tree is contained in a small seed,' says the *Vishnu Purana*, 'so is the whole universe contained in Brahma.'

In rural areas, when the new moon falls on a Monday, the peepal is still worshipped by women, who pour water on its trunk, and lay at its roots a copper coin and sweetmeats.

It is said to be dangerous to lie or cheat beneath a peepal tree, and sometimes to tease shopkeepers they are told that they ought not to plant one in a bazaar. All the same, there are plenty of peepal trees in our bazaars. It is a tree that grows wherever its seed falls; it will take root in a wall or on a rooftop—or even in the fork of another tree if given the chance. As its roots are quite capable of pushing through bricks and mortar, it is best to plant it some distance away from buildings.

No other tree has a leaf which tapers to such a perfect point as the peepal. When it rains, you can see the water drip from the points. Water runs off more easily from a point than from a blunt end, and the sooner a leaf dries the better it is for the tree.

The leaf is beautiful, and has been likened to the perfect male physique. From the stalk (the human neck) the edges of the leaf run squarely out on either side (the shoulders) and then curve round inwards to end in a finely pointed tail (the waist), so that the suggestion is of a square, broad torso upon a narrow waist—a body such as we see in pictures of Krishna.

While the chief occupants of the banyan are various birds and insects, the peepal is said to be the residence of a wide variety of ghosts and mischievous spirits. The most mischievous of these is the Munjia. He lives in lonely peepal trees, and rushes out at tongas, bullock-carts and buses, trying his best to upset them! Our grandmothers still advise us not to yawn when passing under a peepal tree. Should you yawn, it is best to cover your mouth with your hand, or snap your fingers in front of it. 'Otherwise,' says Grandmother, 'the Munjia will rush down your throat and completely ruin your digestion!'

Peepal trees have very long lives. There are some ancient peepals in Hardwar which are even older than the present town, probably as old as the eleventh-century Mayadevi Temple. A peepal tree taken from India to Sri Lanka in 288 BC is still alive and flourishing. Records of its growth were carefully preserved over the centuries, and it must now be over two thousand years old.

To fell a peepal tree was once looked upon as a great sin. On the other hand, anyone who planted a peepal was said to receive the blessings of generations to come.

Let us also earn the blessings of future generations by planting not only more peepal trees— which are quite capable of looking after themselves— but all kinds of trees for shade and shelter, fruit and flower, beauty and utility.

Can you imagine a country without any trees, a country that has become one vast desert? Well, that is what could easily happen here if we keep cutting our trees and forests without bothering to grow others in their place.

Garden of a Thousand Trees

No one in his right mind would want to chop down a mango tree. Every mango tree, even if it grows wild, is generous with its juicy fruit, known sometimes as 'the nectar of the gods', and sometimes as the 'king of fruits'. You can eat ripe mangoes fresh from the tree; you can eat them in pickles or chutneys or jams; you can eat them flattened out and dried, as in aam papad; you can drink the juice with milk as in 'mango-fool'; you can even pound the kernel into flour and use it as a substitute for wheat. And there are over a hundred different varieties of the mango, each with its own distinctive flavour.

But in praising the fruit, let us not forget the tree, for it is one of the stateliest trees in India, its tall, spreading branches a familiar sight throughout the country, from the lower slopes of the Himalayas to Cape Comorin.

In Gujarat, on the night of the seventh of the month of Savan (July-August), a young mango tree is planted near the house and worshipped by the womenfolk to protect their children from disease. Sometimes a post of mango wood is set up when Ganesh is worshipped.

If you live anywhere in the plains of northern India, you will often have seen a grove of giant mango trees, sometimes appearing like an oasis in the midst of the vast, flat countryside. Beneath the trees you may find a well and a small temple. It is here that the tired, dusty farmer sits down to rest and eat his midday chapati, following it with a draught of cold water from the well. If you join him and ask him who planted the mango grove, he will not be able to tell you; it was there when he was a boy, and probably when his father was a boy too. Some mango groves are very, very old.

Have you heard of the Garden of a Thousand Trees? Probably not. But you must have heard of the town of Hazaribagh in Bihar. Well, a huge mango grove containing over a thousand trees—some of which are still there—was known as hazari, and around these trees a village grew, spreading in time into the modern town of Hazaribagh, 'Garden of a Thousand Trees'. Anyway, that's the story you will hear from the oldest inhabitants of the town. And even today, the town is almost hidden in a garden of trees: mango and neem, sal and tamarind.

All are welcome in a mango grove. But during the mango season, when the trees are in fruit, you enter the grove at your own peril! At this time of the year it is watched over by a fierce chowkidar, whose business is to drive away any mischievous children who creep into the grove in the hope of catching him asleep and making off with a few juicy mangoes. The chowkidar is a busy man. Even before the mangoes ripen, he has to battle not only with the village urchins, but also with raiding parties of emerald-green parrots, who swarm all over the trees, biting deep into the green fruit. Sometimes he sits under a tree in the middle of the grove, pulling a rope which makes a large kerosene-tin rattle in the branches. He can try shouting too, but his voice can't compete with the screams of the parrots. They wheel in circles round the grove and, spreading their tails, settle on the topmost branches.

Even when there are no mangoes, you will find parrots in the grove, because during their breeding season, their favourite nesting places are the holes in the gnarled trunks of old mango trees.

Other birds, including the blue jay and the little green coppersmith, favour the mango grove for the same reason. And sometimes you may spot a small owl peering at you from its hole halfway up the trunk of an old tree.

The Silk-Cotton Tree

Most of you, even if you do not play badminton, are familiar with a shuttlecock. Well, if you take a shuttlecock and paint it a bright crimson, you will get a fair idea of what the flower of the semul (or silk-cotton tree) looks like.

Now just imagine a tall, leafless tree covered with masses of crimson flowers, and you will know what this wonderful tree looks like in spring. There are few trees in the world that can compare with it in beauty and brilliance.

You may, of course, have seen a semul tree either in the jungle or along a tree-lined avenue in one of our cities. It is a good shade-tree, losing its leaves for only a brief period, just before it flowers. During the summer months you will find its seeds covered with white cotton, which is blown far and wide by the slightest breeze. This cotton is not suitable for spinning and weaving into cloth, but it is used for stuffing pillows and cushions.

Like most trees, the semul has its place in our folklore. Whenever the Murias, a forest tribe in Madhya Pradesh, found a village, their first act was to plant a semul tree at the centre of the site. There are others who use its wood to make the posts around which couples walk at the marriage ceremony. Images of parrots fashioned from the wood of the semul are also hung in the marriage sheds, for the parrot represents the spirit of the forest.

Semul wood is very soft, and is sometimes used for making toys. Fishermen also use it to make floats for their nets. The seeds are valued as a nourishing food for cattle, while the gum from the bark is used in medicines by Ayurvedic doctors.

The semul is as remarkable for the colour and profusion of its flowers as for the large number of birds that visit it when it is in flower. Some birds come for the nectar which is found in the big, red flowers; some come in search of the thousands of drowned insects which lie at the bottom of the flower cups; some come because the soft wood of the tree can easily be hollowed out for a nesting site. Whatever the reason, from morning till night the tree is full of visitors.

Among those who visit the semul are a large number of crows, who come to have a few sips of the nectar before setting out on the day's mischief. There are mynas of various kinds, squabbling for the best seats. Barbets and bulbuls, king crows and koels, all join in the feasting. In addition to the birds, palm squirrels dart about from place to place, tossing their fluffy tails from side to side, and chattering noisily as they jostle each other on the branches. And all the time flowers are being constantly broken off, falling to the ground with soft thuds.

The rosy pastors or rose-coloured starlings are

probably the most noticeable visitors to the semul tree. They come in flocks, not singly; their colour vies with that of the flowers; and they make such a racket that one thinks that a terrible riot is going on. But the pastors are not fighting, they are simply enjoying themselves.

Another inhabitant of the semul tree is the big Indian bee. This bee lives in huge nests, or combs, which are usually attached to the branches of the semul tree. The straight, horizontal branches of the semul are just right for supporting the huge combs, which can be as much as five feet in length and two and a half feet in width. The residents of the comb are of three kinds—the males or drones who do no work, the females who lay the eggs, and the workers who build the giant combs. These are permanent colonies, filled with honey or wax or pollen.

The sting of the big bee is painful and poisonous, especially in hot weather; but jungle tribes, such as the Kols and the Santals, have developed an immunity to the poison. They don't mind being stung. But strangers to the forests have been badly stung, and it is wise not to disturb these bees, for they will attack both man and beast with great ferocity.

There is the story of two shikaris who were resting between beats one hot May morning in a central Indian jungle. Overhead spread the crown of a tall semul tree with a dozen great combs of the big bee hanging from the branches. One of the shikaris unwisely lit a pipe. Up went the pipe smoke, and down came the bees! They were soon buzzing around the two shikaris, who beat an undignified retreat, running for over a mile across open country until they reached the safety of a river. They were so badly stung that they had to remain in the river for hours, up to their chins in water.

From Small Beginnings

On the first clear September day, towards the end of the rains, I visited the pine knoll, my place of peace and power.

It was months since I'd last been there. Trips to the plains, a crisis in my affairs, involvements with other people and their troubles, and an entire monsoon, had come between me and the grassy, pine-topped slope facing the Hill of Fairies (Pari Tibba to the locals). Now I tramped through late monsoon foliage—tall ferns, bushes festooned with flowering convolvulus—crossed the stream by way of its little bridge of stones and climbed the steep hill to the pine slope.

When the trees saw me, they made as if to turn in my direction. A puff of wind came across the valley from the distant snows. A long-tailed blue magpie took alarm and flew noisily out of an oak tree. The cicadas were suddenly silent. But the trees remembered me. They bowed gently in the breeze and beckoned me nearer, welcoming me home. Three pines, a straggling oak, and a wild cherry. I went among them, acknowledged their welcome with a touch of my hand against their trunks. The oak had been there the longest, and the wind had bent its upper branches and twisted a few, so that it looked shaggy and undistinguished. But, like the philosopher who is careless about his dress and appearance, the oak has secrets, a hidden wisdom. It has learnt the art of survival!

While the oak and the pines are older than me and have been here for many years, the cherry tree is exactly seven years old. I know, because I planted it.

One day I had this cherry seed in my hand, and on an impulse I thrust it into the soft earth, and then went away and forgot all about it. A few months later I found a tiny cherry tree in the long grass. I did not expect it to survive. But the following year it was two feet tall. And then some goats ate its leaves, and a grass cutter's scythe injured the stem, and I was sure it would wither away. But it renewed itself, sprang up even faster; and within three years it was a healthy, growing tree, about five feet tall.

I left the hills for two years—forced by circumstances to make a living in Delhi—but this time I did not forget the cherry tree. I thought about it fairly often, sent telepathic messages of encouragement in its direction. And when, a couple of years ago, I returned in the autumn, my heart did a somersault when I found my tree sprinkled with pale pink blossom. (The Himalayan cherry flowers in November.) And later, when the fruit was ripe, the tree was visited by finches, tits, bulbuls and other small birds, all had come to feast on the sour, red cherries.

Last summer I spent a night on the pine knoll, sleeping on the grass beneath the cherry tree. I lay awake for hours, listening to the chatter of the stream and the occasional tonk-tonk of a nightjar; and watching through the branches overhead, the stars turning in the sky, I felt the power of the sky and earth, and the power of a small cherry seed ...

And so, when the rains are over, this is where I come, so that I might feel the peace and power of this place. It's a big world and momentous events are taking place all the time. But this is where I have seen the most momentous of them all happen.

Sacred Trees

Explore the history and mythology of almost any Indian tree, and you will find that at some period of our civilization it has held an important place in the minds and hearts of the people of this land.

During the rains, when the neem pods fall and

are crushed underfoot, they give out a strong refreshing aroma which lingers in the air for days. This is because the neem gives out more oxygen than most trees. When the ancient herbalists held that the neem was a great purifier of the air, and that its leaves, bark and sap had medicinal qualities, they were quite right, for the neem is still used in medicine today.

From the earliest times it was connected with the gods who protect us from disease. Some castes regarded the tree as sacred to Sitala, the goddess of smallpox. When children fell ill, a branch of the neem was waved over them. The tree is said to have sprung from the nectar of the gods, and people still chew the leaves as a means of purification, both spiritual and physical.

The tree is also connected with the sun, as in the story, 'The Sun in the Neem Tree'. The sun god invited to dinner a man of the Bairagi tribe whose rules forbade him to eat except by daylight. Dinner was late, and as darkness fell, the Bairagi feared he would have to go hungry. But Suraj Narayan, the sun god, descended from a neem tree and continued shining till dinner was over.

Why have so many trees been held sacred, not only in India but the world over?

To early man they were objects of awe and wonder. The mystery of their growth, the movement of their leaves and branches, the way they seemed to die and then come to life again in spring, the sudden growth of the plant from the seed, all these happenings appeared as miracles—as indeed they are! And because of the wonderful growth of a tree, people began to suppose that it was occupied by spirits, and devotion to a tree became devotion to the spirit or tree-god who occupied it.

In *Puck of Pook's Hill*, Kipling wove some wonderful stories, around Puck, the tree-spirit, and the sacred trees of Old England—oak, ash and thorn: 'I came into England with Oak, Ash, and Thorn, and when Oak, Ash and Thorn are gone, I shall go too.'

Among the Gonds of central India, before a man cut a tree he had to beg its pardon for the injury he was about to inflict on it. He would not shake a tree at night because the tree-spirit was asleep and might be disturbed. When a tree had to be felled, the Gonds would pour ghee on the stump, saying: 'Grow thou out of this, O Lord of the Forest, grow into a hundred shoots! May we grow with a thousand shoots.'

The beautiful mahua is a forest tree held sacred by a number of tribes. Early on the wedding morning, before he goes to fetch his bride, the Bagdi bridegroom goes through a mock marriage with a mahua tree. He embraces it and daubs it with vermilion, his right wrist is bound to it with thread, and after he is released from the tree the thread is used to attach a bunch of mahua leaves to his wrist.

Special respect is paid to trees growing near the graves of Muslim saints. Near the tomb of a famous saint, Musa Sohag, at Ahmedabad, there used to be a large old champa tree—perhaps it is still there— the branches of which were hung with glass bangles. Those anxious to have children came and offered bangles to the saint—the number of bangles depending on the means of the supplicant. If the saint favoured a wish, the champa tree snatched up the bangles and wore them on its arms.

Another spectacular tree which has its place in our folklore is the dhak, or palas, which gave its name to the battlefield of Plassey. It has the habit of dropping its leaves when it flowers, the upper and outer branches standing out in sprays of scarlet and orange. The flowers are sometimes used to dye the powder scattered at Holi, the spring festival, and the wood, said to contain the seed of fire, is used in lighting the Holi bonfire. Legend tells us that the sun god aimed an arrow at the earth, and that it took root and became the palas tree.

The babul (or keekar) is not very impressive to look at but it will grow almost anywhere in the plains, and there are a number of old beliefs associated with it. For instance, you can cure fever and headache at a babul tree if you tie seven cotton threads from your left big toe to your head, and from your head to a branch of the tree. Then you must embrace the trunk seven times. Try it sometime. You will be so busy tying threads that you will forget you ever had a headache! And there are no after effects.

Another belief concerning the babul is that if you water it regularly for thirteen days you acquire control over the spirit who occupies it. There is a story about a man at Saharanpur who did this, and when he died and his corpse was taken away for cremation, no sooner was his pyre lit than he got up and walked away!

In the folklore of India, the mango is the 'wish-fulfilling tree'. When you want to make a wish on a mango tree, shut your eyes and get someone to lead you to the tree; then rub mango blossoms in your hands and make your wish. The favour granted lasts only for a year and the charm must be performed again at the next flowering of the tree. In spring, the young leaves and buds symbolize the darts of Manmatha, or Kama-deva, god of love.

Another 'wishing tree', the kalp-vriksha, is an enormous old mulberry that is still cared for at Joshimath in Garhwal. It is said to be the tree beneath which the great Shankaracharya often meditated during his sojourn in the Himalayas. Judging by its girth, it might well be over a thousand years old.

Whole forests have been held sacred, such as that in Berar which was dedicated to a particular temple; no one dared to buy or cut the trees. The sacred groves near Mathura, where Lord Krishna sported as a youth, were also protected for centuries. But now, alas, even the hallowed groves are disappearing, making way for the demands of an ever-increasing population. A pity, because every human needs a tree of his own. Even if you do not worship the tree-spirit, you can love the tree.

Silent Birth

When the earth gave birth to this tree,
There came no sound:
A green shoot thrust
In silence from the ground.
Our births don't come so quiet—
Most lives run riot—
But the bud opens silently,
And flower gives way to fruit.
So must we search
For the stillness within the tree,
The silence within the root.

VI
Flowers

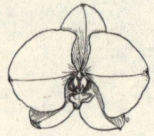

I don't think I could have got through life without the company of flowers. They sustain and stimulate. My desk is just a place of work until one of the children places a vase of flowers upon it, and then it becomes a place of delight. Be it a rose or a chrysanthemum or a simple daisy, it will help me in my work. They are there to remind me that life has its beautiful moments.

When I step out for one of my walks, I look for wild flowers, even the most humble of flowers hiding on the hillside. And if I do not know their names, I invent their names, because it's nice to know someone by his or her name . . .

A New Flower

It was the first day of spring (according to the Hindu calendar), but here in the Himalayas it still seemed mid-winter. A cold wind hummed and whistled through the pines, while dark rain clouds were swept along by the west wind only to be thrust back by the east wind.

I was climbing the steep road to my cottage at the top of the hill when I was overtaken by nine-year-old Usha hurrying back from school. She had tied a scarf round her head to keep her hair from blowing. Dark hair and eyes, and pink cheeks, were all accentuated by the patches of snow still lying on the hillside.

'Look,' she said, pointing, 'a new flower!'

It was a single, butter-yellow blossom, and it stood out like a bright star against the drab winter grass. I hadn't seen anything like it before, and had no idea what its name might be. No doubt its existence was recorded in some botanical tome. But for me it was a new discovery.

What's In a Name

If there is any dishonesty in our natures, sooner or later wild flowers will bring it out. The flowers of our woods and hills are often so difficult to identify that we are tempted to improvise—to find rare plants in places where they do not grow, and to discover other plants that no one has ever heard of. Even botanists make mistakes—unless they are the fanatical types, of whom it has been said that they visit their mothers' graves only to study the plants that grow on them!

To avoid any blunders, I shall confine myself in this short article to some comments on those wild flowers about which there can be little or no controversy. Unfortunately, there is no comprehensive *Flora Himalayensis* available; but as most of the wild flowers growing between six and seven thousand feet in the Himalayas (in the vicinity of our hill stations) are similar to those of the temperate countries, their identification is not too difficult.

Take for instance, the oxalis or wood sorrel. During the rains this plant takes possession of the hill slopes. Its pretty mauve flower set amidst a cluster of heart-shaped leaflets is unmistakable. The Paharis call it khatta-mitha (sour-sweet), because of the mild acidity of its leaves. Cows like it, though too much is supposed to cause diarrhoea; and it is said that the milk of the cow which has eaten the wood sorrel cannot easily be turned into butter. In Europe it was once used in salads. The origin of the Irish shamrock emblem was the leaf of the wood sorrel, but today the leaf of the whole clover (also common in the Himalayas) takes its place.

Another sorrel, though vastly different, grows in our hills. Unlike the modest oxalis, the sheep sorrel is a tough weed, growing from rocks, the walls of old houses, and in soils which refuse to support any other plant life. The flowers, which come out in spring and autumn, are pink flaky things, rather like confetti. They, too, are acidic (in fact, sorrel means sour), and though sheep sorrel may have been thought fit only for sheep, its near-relative, sorrel dock, was once eaten along with mutton.

John Ruskin in one of his bad moods said that plants were named, some from diseases, some from vermin, some from blockheads (meaning botanists), and the rest anyhow. Certainly names can be confusing. The cherry used to be called the merry. Merry is a false singular from the French merise (wild cherry), as cherry is from cerise. The gooseberry is known in India as the *rus*berry, which is likely to be confused with raspberries.

A plant may deceive us by its name, even its botanical name. If it is something which has montana or mountain in its name, the chances are it grows in a low valley. (Or perhaps mountains have grown in size since Christian, in the *Pilgrim's Progress*, saw 'a wide field, full of dark mountains'.) The winter jasmine flowers in the Himalayas in spring. The 'basant' or spring flower, is more common in the depths of winter. There must be some twenty kinds of daisies, and ten varieties of dandelions, and in trying to tell one from the other, the amateur botanist is tempted to cry, 'A plague on both your houses!'

Some flowers are easily recognized. The dog rose is unmistakable, growing wild on the hills in spring. Why so unlovely a name? Because it is the translation of the flower's Greek name which means a cure for hydrophobia. Our forebears studied and gathered wild flowers and plants not so much for their beauty as for their medicinal or food value. Such plants were known as 'simples'—that existed before the physician devised 'compounds'. The plants themselves often indicated their usefulness: a walnut, having a hard shell like a skull and a kernel configured like a brain, signified that it was a cure for all troubles of the head!'

Some plants are still better known by their usefulness (or harmfulness) than by their appearance. When we speak of tobacco, we do not think of its lovely flower. Nor can we visualize the onion as a lily. But it belongs to the lily family, as does the leek.

'What lovely flowers!' I exclaimed, pointing to a corner of a friend's garden. 'What are they?'

'Potatoes,' was the reply. And potatoes do have

lovely flowers. They also belong to the poisonous nightshade family!

It is so easy for the flower enthusiast to blunder when it comes to distinguishing types and families of flowers. Botanists have certainly done their best to confuse the nature lover. But we should not allow ourselves to be discouraged; we have as much right to the enjoyment of wild flowers as they.

What's in a name? Forget-me-not is more expressive than *Myosotis*. Lady's bedstraw has more charm than *Galium verum*, and dandelion is far sweeter than *Taraxacum officinale*. I do not know what the Pahari names are for these flowers, but they grow in our hills and are there to be enjoyed. (And dandelion flowers make excellent wine!) Let not their names blind us to their beauty and mystery; but let us wonder, like Tennyson, at their miraculous presence:

> Flower in the crannied wall,
> I pluck you out of the crannies,
> I hold you here, root and all, in my hand,
> Little flower—but if I could understand
> What you are, root and all, and all in all,
> I should know what God and man are.

Flowers Wild and Tame

The cosmos has all the genius of simplicity. The plant stands tall and erect; its foliage is uncomplicated; its inflorescences are bold, fresh, cheerful. Any flower, from a rose to a rhododendron, can be complicated. The cosmos is splendidly simple.

No wonder it takes its name from the Greek cosmos, meaning the universe as an ordered whole—the sum total of experience! For this unpretentious flower does seem to sum it all up: perfection without apparent striving for it, the artistry of the South American footballer! Needless to say, it came from tropical America.

And growing it is no trouble. A handful of seeds thrown in a waste patch or on a grassy hill slope, and a few months later there they are, en masse, doing their samba in the sunshine. They are almost wild, but not quite. They need very little attention, but if you take them too much for granted they will go away the following year. Simple they may be, but not insensitive. They need plenty of space. And as my own small apartment cannot accommodate them, they definitely belong to my dream garden.

My respect for the cosmos goes back to my childhood when I wandered into what seemed like a forest of these flowers, all twice my height (I must have been five at the time) but looking down on me in the friendliest way, their fine feathery foliage giving off a faint aroma. Now when I find them flowering on the hillsides in mellow October sunshine, they are like old friends and I greet them accordingly, pressing my face to their petals.

Not everyone likes the cosmos. I have met some upper-class ladies (golf-club members) who complain that it gives them hay fever, and they use this as an excuse to root out all cosmos from their gardens. I expect they are just being snobbish. There are other flowers which give off just as much pollen dust.

I have noticed the same snobbishness in regard to marigolds, especially the smaller Indian variety. 'Cultivated' people won't cultivate these humble but attractive flowers. Is it because they are used for making garlands? Or because they are not delicately scented? Or because they are so easily grown in the backyards of humble homes?

My grandparents once went to war with each other over the marigold. Grandfather had grown a few in one corner of the garden. Just as they began flowering, they vanished—Granny had removed them overnight! There was a row, and my grandparents did not speak to each other for several days. Then, by calling them 'French' marigolds, Grandfather managed to reintroduce them to the garden. Granny liked the idea of having something 'French' in her garden. Such is human nature!

Sometimes a wild flower can put its more spectacular garden cousins to shame. I am thinking now of the commelina, which I discover in secret places after the rains have passed. Its bright skyblue flowers take my breath away. It has a sort of unguarded innocence that is beyond corruption.

Wild roses give me more pleasure than the sophisticated domestic variety. On a walk in the Himalayan foothills I have encountered a number of these shrubs and climbers—the ineptly named dog rose, sparkling white in summer; the sweet briar with its deep pink petals and bright red rose hips; the trailing rose, found in shady places; and the wild raspberry (the fruit more attractive than the flower) which belongs to the same family.

A sun lover, I like plenty of yellow on the hillsides and in gardens—sunflowers, Californian poppies, winter jasmine, St John's wort, buttercups, wild strawberries, mustard in bloom . . . But if you live in a hot place, you might prefer cooling blues and soft purples—forget-me-nots, bluebells, cornflowers, lavender.

I'd go far for a sprig of sweetly-scented lavender. This tame-looking, blue-green, stiff, sticky, and immovable shrub holds as much poetry and romance in its wiry arms as would fill a large book. Most cultivated flowers were originally wild and many take their names from the botanists who first 'tamed' them. Thus, the dahlia is named after Mr Dahl, a Swede; the rudbeckia after Rudbeck, a Dutchman; the zinnia after Dr Zinn, a German; and the lobelia after Monsieur Lobel, a Flemish physician. They and others brought to Europe many of the flowers they found growing wild in tropical America, Asia and Africa.

But I am no botanist. I prefer to be the butterfly, perfectly happy in going from flower to flower in search of nectar.

Some Plants Become Friends

The little rose begonia: it has a glossy chocolate leaf, a pretty rose-pink flower, and it grows and flowers in my bedroom—almost all the year round. What more can one ask for?

Some plants become friends. Most garden flowers are fair-weather friends; gone in the winter when times are difficult up here in the mountains. Those who stand by you in adversity—plant or human—are your true friends; there aren't many around, so cherish them and take care of them in all seasons.

A loyal plant friend is the variegated ivy that has spread all over my bedroom wall. My small bedroom-cum-study gets plenty of light and sun, and when the windows are open, cool breeze from the mountains floats in, rustling the leaves of the ivy. (This breeze can turn into a raging blizzard in winter—on one occasion, even blowing the roof away—but right now, it's just a zephyr, gentle and balmy.) Ivy plants seem to like my room, and this one, which I brought up from Dehra, took an instant liking to my desk and walls, so that I now have difficulty keeping it from trailing over my typewriter when I am at work.

I like to take in other people's sick or discarded plants and nurse or cajole them back to health. This has given me a bit of a reputation as a plant doctor. Actually, all I do is give an ailing plant a quiet corner where it can rest and recuperate from whatever ails it—they have usually been ill-treated in some way. Plant abuse, no less! And it's wonderful how quickly a small tree or plant will recover if given a little encouragement.

I rescued a dying asparagus fern from the portals of the Savoy Hotel, and now, six months later, its strong feathery fronds have taken over most of one window, so that I have no need of curtains. Nandu, the owner of Savoy, now wants his fern back.

Maya Banerjee's sick geranium, never allowed to settle in one place—hence its stunted appearance—has, within a fortnight of being admitted to my plant ward, burst forth in such an array of new leaf and flower that I'm afraid it might pull a muscle or strain a ligament from too much activity.

Should I return these and other plants when they have fully recovered? I don't think they want to go back. And I should hate to see them suffering relapses on being returned to their former abodes. So I tell the owners that their plants need monitoring for a while ... Perhaps, if I sent in doctor's bills, the demands for their return would not be so strident?

Loyalty in plants, as in friends, must be respected and rewarded. If dandelions show a tendency to do well on the steps of the house, then that is where they shall be encouraged to grow. If a sorrel is happier on the window sill than on the hillside, then I shall let it stay, even if it means the window won't close properly. And if the hydrangea does better in my neighbour's garden than mine, then my neighbour shall be given the hydrangea. Among flower lovers, there must be no double standards: generosity, not greed; sugar, not spite.

And what of the rewards for me, apart from the soothing effect of fresh fronds and leaves at my place of work and rest? Well, the other evening I came home to find my room vibrating to the full-throated chorus of several crickets who had found the ivy to their liking. I thought they would keep me up all night with their music; but when I switched the light off, they immediately fell silent. So, crickets don't sing in the dark, I surmised, and switched the light on again. Once more, I was treated to symphonic variations on a theme by Tchaikovsky.

This reminded me that I hadn't listened to Tchaikovsky for some time, so I played a tape of 'The Dance of the Sugar Plum Fairy' from the

Nutcracker Suite. The crickets maintained a respectful silence, even with the lights on.

My Flower of the Month

The dandelion growing on my retaining wall must be my flower of the month. It asserts its right to be there, where practically nothing else will flourish. Without any care or nourishment, it survives and grows strong and upright. Pluck it if you will, but there's no uprooting it from that space between two stones where it is so firmly embedded.

The dandelion opens its petals to the first rays of the sun and closes when the sunlight fades. And it is called love's oracle because of the custom of blowing on its puffball of seeds to discover whether 'she loves me' or 'she loves me not'. I have always been able to regulate my breath so as to obtain the answer I wanted!

My flower of the month, when the dandelion is not in bloom, is the poppy, while it lasts. A classic flower, it is extravagantly beautiful. The scarlet poppy is the most showy but I like the plain white one as it makes for such a pleasing contrast, a pattern of poppies.

The unseasonal showers we have been having

give today's poppies a rather bedraggled look, but there will be fresh blooms tomorrow.

There's an old saying: 'Pluck poppies, make thunder.'

A wild species of geranium (the round-leafed cranesbill, to give its English name) with a tiny lilac flower, has responded to my overtures, making a great display in a tub where I encouraged it to spread. Never one to spurn a gesture of friendship, I have given it the freedom of the shady back veranda. Let it be my flower of the month, this rainy August.

The Scent of the Snapdragon

I would be the last person to belittle a flower because of its colour or appearance, but it does happen that my favourites are those with their own distinctive fragrance.

The rose, of course, is a joy to all—even to my baby granddaughter, who enjoys taking one apart, petal by petal—but there are other less-spectacular blooms, which have a lovely and sometimes elusive fragrance all their own.

I have a special fondness for snapdragons. If I sniff hard at them, I don't catch any scent at all.

They seem to hold it back from me. But if I walk past a bed of these flowers, or even a single plant, the gentlest of fragrances is wafted to me, zephyr-like. And if I stop to try and take it all in, it goes again! I find this quite tantalizing, but it has given me a special regard for this modest flower.

The bees love the snapdragon—the antirrhinum—as much as I do. I have seen honeybees push their way through the pursed lips of the antirrhinum and disappear completely. A few minutes later they stagger out again, bottoms first.

Carnations, with their strong scent of cloves, are great show-offs. And here, in India, the jasmine can be rather heady and overpowering. The honeysuckle, too, insists on making its presence known. There is a honeysuckle creeper outside the study window of my cottage in the hills, and all through the summer its sweet, rather cloying fragrance drifts in through the open window. It is delightful at times; but at other times I have to close the window so that I can give my attention to other, less intrusive, smells—like the soft scent of petunias (another of my favourites) near the doorstep, and pine needles on the hillside, and great bunches of sweet peas placed on my table.

Some flowers can be quite tricky. One would think that the calendula had no scent at all. Certainly the flower gives nothing away. But run your fingers gently over the leaves and then bring them to your face, and you will be touched, just briefly, by the most delicate of aromas.

Sometimes leaves outdo their blooms. The lemon geranium, for instance, is valued more for its fragrant leaves than for its rather indeterminate flowers. It is the same with verbena. And I cannot truthfully say what ordinary mint looks like in flower. The refreshing aroma of its leaves, when crushed, makes up for any absence of floral display.

Not all plants are fragrant. Some, like the asafoetida, will keep strong men at bay. Of course, one man's fragrance might well turn out to be another creature's bad smell. Geraniums, my grandmother insisted, kept snakes away because they couldn't stand the smell of these flowers. She surrounded her north Indian bungalow with pots of geraniums. It's true we never found a snake in the house, so she may have been right!

But snakes must like some smells, close to the ground, or by now they'd have taken to living in more elevated places; but I am told their sense of smell is rather dull. When I lie on summer grass in the Himalayas, I am conscious of the many good smells around me—the grass itself, redolent of the morning's dew; bruised clover; wild violets; tiny buttercups and golden stars and strawberry flowers and many I shall never know the names of . . .

And here are some flower haikus (well, almost!) I wrote last summer:

Blossom Time

Poinsettia

Bright red
The poinsettia flames
As autumn and the old year wanes.

Ferns

Shaded in a deep ravine
The ferns are upright, dark and green.

Jasmine Time

Jasmine flowers in her hair,
Jasmine scents are everywhere.
Languid summer days are here;
There's sweet longing in the air.

Geranium

Red geranium
Gleaming against the polished floor:
Memory, hold the door!

Rose of Harsil

Her beauty brought her fame.
But only the wild rose growing beside her grave
Was there to hear that whispered name:
Gulabi.

Begonia

There's a begonia in her cheeks,
Pink as the flush of early dawn
On Sikkim's peaks.

Snapdragon

Antirrhinums line the wall,
Sturdy little dragons all!

Petunias

Petunias I must praise—
Their soft perfume
Takes me by surprise!

Rose of Tibet

Take thou this rose, but don't forget
The wild red rose of old Tibet.

VII
Rain

'Raindrops keep falling on my head' and other songs testify to the effect that rain has on poets and song writers. In my debut novel, Rusty discovers the sensual delights of bathing in the first monsoon rain after the scorching Indian summer. And the scents and sounds of rain have been part of several of my novels, stories and essays since then.

India is all about waiting for the rain to come, and then waiting for it to go. Hence the proverb:

When the floods come up the fish eat ants;
When the floods go down the ants eat fish.

Barsaat

The onset of the monsoon has always been my favourite time of the year. Like every Indian, I am more keenly alive to the monsoon than to any other season. This is as true of me today as it was in the fifties, when I was a young boy. Rusty's experience of the first rains in The Room on the Roof *is also my own:*

Dust. It blew up in great clouds, swirling down the road, clutching and clinging to everything it touched—burning, choking, stinging dust.

Then thunder.

The wind dropped suddenly, there was a hushed expectancy in the air. And then, out of the dust came big black rumbling clouds.

Something was happening.

At first there was a lonely drop of water on the window sill, then a patter on the roof. Rusty felt a thrill of anticipation, and a mountain of excitement. The rains had come to break the monotony of the summer months—the monsoon had arrived!

The sky shuddered, the clouds groaned, a fork of lightning struck across the sky, and then the sky itself exploded.

The rain poured down, drumming on the corrugated roof. Rusty's vision was reduced to about twenty yards; it was as though the room had been cut off from the rest of the world by an impenetrable wall of water.

The rains had arrived, and Rusty wanted to experience, to the full, the novelty of that first shower. He threw off his clothes and ran naked on to the roof, and the wind sprang up and whipped the water across his body so that he writhed in ecstasy. The rain was more intoxicating than the alcohol, and it was with difficulty that he restrained himself from shouting and dancing in mad abandon. The force and freshness of the rain brought tremendous relief, washed away the stagnation that had been settling on him, poisoning his mind and body.

The rain swept over the town, cleansing the sky and the earth. The trees bent beneath the force of wind and water. The field was a bog, flowers flattened to the ground.

Rusty returned to the room, exhilarated, his body weeping. He was confronted by a flood. The water had come in through the door and the window and the skylight, and the floor was flooded ankle-deep. He took to his bed.

The bed took on the glamour of a deserted island in the middle of the ocean. He dried himself on the sheets, conscious of a warm, sensuous glow. Then he sat on his haunches and gazed out through the window.

The rain thickened, the tempo quickened. There was the banging of a door, the swelling of a gutter, the staccato splutter of the rain rhythmically persistent on the roof. The drainpipe coughed and choked, the curtain flew to its limit; the lean trees swayed and bowed with the burden of wind and weather. The road was a rushing torrent, the gravel path inundated with little rivers. The monsoon had arrived!

But the rain stopped as unexpectedly as it had begun.

Suddenly it slackened, dwindled to a shower, petered out. Stillness. The dripping of water from the drainpipe drilled into the drain. Frogs croaked, hopping around in the slush.

The sun came out with a vengeance. On leaves and petals, drops of water sparkled like silver and gold. A cat emerged from a dry corner of the building, blinking sleepily, unperturbed and enthusiastic.

The children came running out of their houses.

'Barsaat, barsaat!' they shouted. 'The rains have come!'

The rains had come. And the roof became a

general bathing place. The children, the nightwatchmen, the dogs, all trooped up the steps to sample the novelty of a freshwater shower on the roof.

The maidan became alive with footballs. The game was called monsoon football, it was played in slush, in mud that was ankle-deep; and the football was heavy and slippery and difficult to kick with bare feet. The bazaar youths played barefoot because, in the first place, boots were too cumbersome for monsoon football, and in the second place, they couldn't be afforded.

But the rains brought Rusty only a momentary elation just as the first shower had seemed fiercer and fresher than those which followed; for now it rained every day . . .

Nothing could be more depressing than the dampness, the mildew, and the sunless heat that wrapped itself round the steaming land. Had Somi or Kishen been with Rusty, he might have derived some pleasure from the elements; had Ranbir been with him, he might have found adventure. But alone, he found only boredom.

He spent an idle hour watching the slow dripping from the pipe outside the door.

The Magic of the Monsoon

When I was living in Delhi in the late 1950s, I made occasional forays into nearby towns. Meerut was one of the towns I travelled to, and there, one evening, I saw the magic of the monsoon.

I was staying at a small hotel. There had been no rain for a month, but the atmosphere was humid, there were clouds overhead, dark clouds burgeoning with moisture. Thunder blossomed in the air.

The monsoon was going to break that day. I knew it, the birds knew it, the grass knew it. There was the smell of rain in the air. And the grass, the birds and I responded to this odour with the same sensuous longing.

A large drop of water hit the window sill, darkening the thick dust on the woodwork. A faint breeze had sprung up, and again I felt the moisture, closer and warmer.

Then the rain approached like a dark curtain.

I could see it marching down the street, heavy and remorseless. It drummed on the corrugated tin roof and swept across the road and over the balcony of my room. I sat there without moving, letting the rain soak my sticky shirt and gritty hair.

Outside, the street rapidly became empty. The crowd dissolved in the rain. Then buses, cars and bullock-carts ploughed through the suddenly rushing water. A group of small boys, gloriously naked, came romping along a side street, which was like a river in spate. A garland of marigolds, swept off the steps of a temple, came floating down the middle of the road.

The rain stopped as suddenly as it had begun. The day was dying, and the breeze remained cool and moist. In the brief twilight that followed, I was witness to the great yearly flight of insects into the cool brief freedom of the night.

Termites and white ants, which had been sleeping through the hot season, emerged from their lairs. Out of every hole and crack, and from under the roots of trees, huge winged ants emerged, fluttering about heavily on this, the first and last flight of their lives. There was only one direction in which they could fly—towards the light, towards the street lights and the bright neon tube light above my balcony.

The light above the balcony attracted a massive quivering swarm of clumsy termites, giving the impression of one thick, slowly revolving mass. A frog had found its way through the bathroom and came hopping across the balcony to pause beneath the light. All he had to do was gobble, as insects fell around him.

This was the hour of the geckos, the wall lizards. They had their reward for weeks of patient waiting. Playing their sticky pink tongues, they devoured insects as swiftly and methodically as children devour popcorn. For hours they crammed their stomachs, knowing that such a feast would not come their way again. Throughout the entire hot season the insect world had prepared for this flight out of darkness into light, and the phenomenon would not happen again for another year.

In hot up-country towns in India it is good to have the first monsoon showers arrive at night, while you are sleeping on the veranda. You wake up to the scent of wet earth and fallen neem leaves, and find that a hot and stuffy bungalow has been converted into a cool, damp place. The swish of the banana fronds and the drumming of the rain on broad-leaved sal trees soothes the most fevered brow.

During the rains the frogs have a perfect country music festival. There are two sets of them, it seems, and they sing antiphonal chants all evening, each group letting the other take its turn in the fairest manner. No one sees or hears them during the hot weather, but the moment the monsoon breaks they swarm all over the place.

When night comes on, great moths fly past, and beetles of all shapes and sizes come whirring in at the open windows. Recently, when Prem closed my window to keep out these winged visitors, I remonstrated, saying that as a nature lover I would share my room with them. I'd forgotten that I am inclined to sleep with my mouth open. In the wee hours I woke up, spluttering and choking, to find that I had almost swallowed a large and somewhat unpleasant-tasting moth. I closed the window. Moths are lovely creatures, but a good night's sleep is even lovelier.

At night the fireflies light up their lamps, flashing messages to each other through the mango groves. Some nocturnal insects thrive mainly at the expense of humans. Sometimes one wakes up to find thirty or forty mosquitoes looking through the net in a bloodthirsty manner. If you are sleeping out, you will need that mosquito net.

The road outside is lined with fine babul trees, now covered with powdery little balls of yellow blossom, filling the air with a faint scent. After the first showers there is a great deal of water around, and for many miles the trees are standing in it. The common monsoon sights along an up-country road are often picturesque—the wide plains, with great herds of smoke-coloured, delicate-limbed cattle being driven slowly home for the night, accompanied by troops of ungainly buffaloes and flocks of black long-tailed sheep. Then you come to a pond, where the buffaloes are indulging in a sensuous wallow, no part of them visible but the tips of their noses.

Within a few days of the first rain the air is full of dragonflies, crossing and re-crossing, poised motionless for a moment, then darting away with that mingled grace and power which is unmatched among insects. Dragonflies are the swallows of the insect world; their prey is the mosquito, the gnat, the midge and the fly. These swarms, therefore, tell us that the moistened surface of the ground, with its mouldering leaves and sodden grass, has become one vast incubator teeming with every form of ephemeral life.

After the monotony of a fierce sun and a dusty landscape quivering in the dim distance, one welcomes these days of mild light, green earth, and purple hills coming nearer in the clear and transparent air.

And later on, when the monsoon begins to break up and the hills are dappled with light and shade, dark islands of cloud moving across the bright green sea, the effect on one's spirits is strangely exhilarating.

A Short Monsoon Diary

June 24

The first day of monsoon mist. And it's strange how all the birds fall silent as the mist comes climbing up the hill. Perhaps that's what makes the mist so melancholy; not only does it conceal the hills, it blankets them in silence too. Only an hour ago the trees were ringing with birdsong. And now the forest is deathly still, as though it were midnight.

Through the mist Bijju is calling to his sister. I can hear him running about on the hillside but I cannot see him.

June 25

Some genuine early-monsoon rain, warm and humid, and not that cold high-altitude stuff we've been having all year. The plants seem to know it too, and the first cobra lily rears its head from the ferns as I walk up to the bank and post office.

The mist affords a certain privacy.

A schoolboy asked me to describe the hill station and valley in one sentence, and all I could say was: 'A paradise that might have been.'

June 27

The rains have heralded the arrival of some seasonal visitors—a leopard, and several thousand leeches.

Yesterday afternoon the leopard lifted a dog from near the servants' quarter below the school. In the evening it attacked one of Bijju's cows but fled at the approach of Bijju's mother, who came screaming imprecations.

As for the leeches, I shall soon get used to a little bloodletting every day. Bijju's mother sat down in the shrubbery to relieve herself, and later discovered two fat black leeches feeding on her fair round bottom. I told her she could use one of the spare bathrooms downstairs. But she prefers the wide open spaces.

Other new arrivals are the scarlet minivets (the females are yellow), flitting silently among the leaves like brilliant jewels. No matter how leafy the trees, these brightly coloured birds cannot conceal themselves, although, by remaining absolutely silent, they sometimes contrive to go unnoticed. Along come a pair of drongos, unnecessarily aggressive, chasing the minivets away.

A tree creeper moves rapidly up the trunk of the oak tree, snapping up insects all the way. Now that the rains are here, there is no dearth of food for the insectivorous birds.

August 2
All night the rain has been drumming on the corrugated tin roof. There has been no storm, no thunder, just the steady swish of a tropical downpour. It helps me to lie awake; at the same time, it doesn't keep me from sleeping.

It is a good sound to read by—the rain outside, the quiet within—and, although tin roofs are given to springing unaccountable leaks, there is a feeling of being untouched by, and yet in touch with, the rain.

August 3
The rain stops. The clouds begin to break up, the sun strikes the steep hill on my left. A woman is chopping up sticks. I hear the tinkle of cowbells. In the oak tree, a crow shakes the raindrops from his

feathers and caws disconsolately. Water drips from a leaking drainpipe. And suddenly, clear and pure, the song of the whistling thrush emerges like a dark sweet secret from the depths of the ravine.

August 12

Endless rain, and a permanent mist. We haven't seen the sun for eight or nine days. Everything damp and soggy. Nowhere to go. Pace the room, look out of the window at a few bobbing umbrellas. At least it isn't cold rain. The hillsides are lush as late-monsoon flowers begin to appear—wild balsam, dahlias, begonias and ground orchids.

August 31

It is the last day of August, and the lush monsoon growth has reached its peak. The seeds of the cobra lily are turning red, signifying that the rains are coming to an end.

In a few days the ferns will start turning yellow, but right now they are still firm, green and upright. Ground orchids, mauve lady's slipper and the white butterfly orchids put on a fashion display on the grassy slopes of Landour. Wild dahlias, red, yellow and magenta, rear their heads from the rocky crevices where they have taken hold.

Snakes and rodents, flooded out of their holes and burrows, take shelter in roofs, attics and godowns. A shrew, weak of eyesight, blunders about the rooms, much to the amusement of the children.

'Don't kill it,' admonishes their grandmother. 'Chuchundars are lucky—they bring money!'

And sure enough, I receive a cheque in the mail. Not a very large one, but welcome all the same.

October 3
We have gone straight from monsoon into winter rain. Snow at higher altitudes.

After an evening hailstorm, the sky and hills are suffused with a beautiful golden light.

January 26
Winter Rain in the Hills

In the hushed silence of the house
when I am quite alone, and my friend, who was
    here,
has gone, it is very lonely, very quiet,
as I sit in a liquid silence, a silence within,
surrounded by the rhythm of rain,
the steady drift
of water on leaves, on lemons, on roof,
drumming on drenched dahlias and window
    panes,
while the mist holds the house in a dark caress.

As I pause near a window, the rain stops.
And starts again.
And the trees, no longer green but grey,
menace me with their loneliness.

March 23

Late March. End of winter.

The blackest cloud I've ever seen squatted over Mussoorie, and then it hailed marbles for half an hour. Nothing like a hailstorm to clear the sky. Even as I write, I see a rainbow forming.

VIII
The Winged Ones

Why do car horns jangle the nerves but birdsongs never? I suppose it's the difference between artificial man-made noise and the harmonious sounds of nature. Even insects sing in harmony.

If I burst into a song, all the birds fly away. So I have learnt to remain silent. To live in harmony with nature we must become good listeners . . .

Birds of the Night

Having for a number of years suffered from rather poor vision, I am not the most eagle-eyed of birdwatchers. But, like many who don't see too well, I have good powers of hearing, awakening in the night at the squeak of a mouse or the fluttering of a moth against the window pane. And when, at times, sleep is elusive, I can lie awake and derive pleasure from the sounds and calls of those birds who live largely by night.

Not that all bird-calls are pleasing to the ear. The hawk-cuckoo semitones until one begins to think that the performer must surely burst. But the brainfever bird never bursts. Its cry is repeated for hours at a stretch.

He is a hot-weather bird who haunts the groves and gardens in almost all parts of the country, his range extending from the Himalayan foothills to Cape Comorin. Only Assam and Punjab appear to be free from the attentions of this cuckoo.

Another cuckoo, the common Indian cuckoo, has quite a pleasant note, which may be rendered by the words 'wherefore, wherefore,' with quite a musical cadence. It begins to call about two hours before sunset, and continues through the night until the morning hours. It is usually silent during the middle of the day, when presumably it rests its vocal chords.

There is a third night-loving cuckoo, the koel, who, like the brainfever bird, is not very popular with those who must try to sleep within hearing distance. His 'ku-oo' grows more strident with each successive rise in scale until sleep becomes almost impossible for anyone in the vicinity. Cunningham described it as a 'highly pitched, trisyllabic cry, repeated many times in ascending', as Douglas Dewar writes, 'the jaded dweller in the plains, uttering strange oaths, rushes for his gun and seeks out the disturber of his slumber'. But the clamour breaks off abruptly, and the sleeper returns to bed, rejoicing in the thought that the wretched bird has choked itself. And it is just then that the bird begins all over again!

Nightjars are not much to look at by day, so this short-sighted birdwatcher isn't missing much. But their sounds are distinctive. Douglas Dewar described the call of the Indian nightjar memorably as 'the sound made by a stone skimming over ice'. The nightjar called Horsfield's, most commonly found in Mussoorie, makes a noise similar to that made by striking a plank with a hammer.

We mustn't forget the owls, those most celebrated of night birds, much maligned by poets obsessed with death and cemeteries.

Actually the owls have the pleasantest of calls. The little jungle owlet has a note which is both mellow and musical. Then there is the little scops owl, who speaks only in monosyllables, except for an occasional 'wow'.

Probably the most familiar of Indian owls is the spotted owlet. He is really a noisy bird, who pours forth a volley of chuckles and squeaks and chatters in the early evening and at intervals throughout the night. In the daytime, like other owls, the spotted owlet is silent, and hides away in some dark corner, such as a hole in a tree or a wall, emerging towards sunset to hunt for prey—chiefly insects, but also occasionally mice, shrews and lizards.

Birdsong in the Mountains

Birdwatching is more difficult in the hills than in the plains. It is hard to spot many birds against the dark trees of the varying shades of the hillside.

There are few birds who remain silent for long, however, and one learns of their presence from their calls or songs. Birdsong is with you wherever you go in the Himalayas, from the foothills to the treeline; and it is often easier to recognize a bird from its voice than from its colourful but brief appearance.

The barbet is one of those birds which are heard

more often than they are seen. It has a monotonous, far-reaching call, 'pee-oh, pee-oh', which carries for about a mile. Like politicians, these birds love listening to their own voices, and often two or three will answer each other from different trees, each trying to outdo the rest in a shrill shouting match. Some people like the barbet's call and consider it both striking and pleasant. Some just find it striking.

Hodgson's grey-headed flycatcher-warbler is a long name that ornithologists, in their infinite wisdom, have given to a very small bird. This tiny warbler is heard, if not seen, more often than any other bird throughout the western Himalayas. Its voice is heard in every second tree, and yet there are few who can say what it looks like. Its song (if you can call it that), is not very tuneful and puts me in mind of the notice that sometimes appeared in salons out West: 'The audience is requested not to throw things at the pianist. He is doing his best.'

Our little warbler does its best, incessantly emitting four or five unmusical, but nevertheless joyful and penetrating notes.

Another tiny bird heard more often than it is seen is the green-backed tit, a smart little fellow about the size of a sparrow. It utters a sharp, rather metallic, but not unpleasant call which sounds like 'kiss me, kiss me, kiss me'.

A real songster is the grey-winged ouzel, found here in the Garhwal hills. Throughout the early summer it makes the wooded hillsides ring with a melody that Nelson Eddy would have been proud of. Joining in sometimes with a sweet song of its own, is the green pigeon. As though to mock their arias, the laughing-thrushes, who are exponents of heavy rock, give vent to some weird calls of their own.

When I first came to live in the hills, it was the song of the Himalayan whistling-thrush that first caught my attention. I was sitting at my window, gazing out at the new leaves on the walnut tree. All was still; the wind was at peace with itself, the mountains brooded massively under a darkening sky. Then, emerging like a sweet secret from the depths of a deep ravine, came this indescribably beautiful call.

It is a song that never fails to enchant me. The birds starts with a hesitant whistle, as though trying out the tune; then, confident of the melody, it bursts into full song, a crescendo of sweet notes and variations ringing clearly across the hillside. Suddenly the song breaks off, right in the middle of a cadenza, and I am left wondering what happened to make the bird stop. Nothing really, because the song is taken up again a few moments later.

One day I saw the whistling-thrush perched on the broken garden fence. He was a deep, glistening purple, his shoulders flecked with white. He had sturdy black legs and a strong yellow beak; a dapper fellow who would have looked just right in a top hat. As time passed, he 'grew accustomed to my face' and became a regular visitor to the garden. On sultry summer afternoons I would find him flapping about in the water tank. Later, refreshed and sunning himself on the roof, he would treat me to a little concert before flying off to his shady ravine.

It was a boy from the next village who acquainted me with the legend of the whistling-thrush. According to the story, the young god, Krishna, fell asleep near a stream, and while he slept a small boy made off with Krishna's famous flute. Upon waking and finding his flute gone, Krishna was so angry that he changed the culprit into a bird. But having once playing on the flute, the boy had learnt bits and pieces of the god's enchanting music. And so he continued, in his disrespectful way, to play the music of the gods, only stopping now and then (as the whistling-thrush does), when he couldn't remember the tune.

It wasn't long before my whistling-thrush was joined by a female. Sometimes they gave solo performances, sometimes they sang duets; and these latter notes, no doubt, were love calls, because it wasn't long before the pair were making forays into the rocky ledges of the ravine, looking for a suitable nesting site.

The birds were liveliest in midsummer; but even in the depths of winter, with snow lying on the ground, they would suddenly start singing, as they flitted from pine to oak to naked chestnut.

The wild cherry tree, which grows just outside my bedroom window, attracts a great many small birds, both when it is in flower and when it is in fruit.

When it is covered with small pink blossoms, the most common visitor is a little yellow-backed sunbird, who emits a squeaky little song as she flits from branch to branch. She extracts the nectar from the blossoms with her long tubular tongue.

Amongst other visitors are the flycatchers, gorgeous birds, especially the paradise flycatcher with its long white tail and ghost-like flight. Basically an insect eater, it likes fruits for dessert, and will visit the tree when the cherries are ripening. While moving alone the boughs of the tree, they utter twittering notes, with occasional louder calls, and now and then the male breaks into a sweet little song, thus justifying the name shah bulbul (king of the nightingales), by which he is known in northern India.

At the Bird Bath

A whistling-thrush comes to bathe in the rainwater puddle beneath the window. He loves this spot. So now, when there is no rain, I fill the puddle with water, so that my favourite bird keeps coming.

His bath finished, he perches on a branch of the walnut tree. His glossy blue-black wings glitter in the sunshine. At any moment he will start singing.

Here he goes! He tries out the tune, whistling to himself, and then, confident of the notes, sends his thrilling full-throated voice far over the forest. The song dies down, trembling, lingering in the air; starts again, joyfully, and then suddenly stops, as though the singer had forgotten the words or the tune.

A little distance from my home, a number of small birds bathe and drink in the little pool beneath the cherry tree: hunting parties of tits—grey tits, red-headed tits and green-backed tits, and two delicate little willow-warblers. They take turns in the pool. While the green-backs are taking a plunge, the red-heads wait patiently on the moss-covered rocks, coming down later to sip daintily at the edge of the pool; they don't like getting their feet wet! Finally, when they have all gone away, the whistling-thrush arrives and indulges in an orgy of bathing, as he now has the entire pool to himself.

The babblers are adept at snapping up the little garden skinks that scuttle about in the leaves and the grass. The skinks are quite brittle and are easily broken to pieces with a few hard raps of the beak. Then down they go! Babblers are also good at sifting through dead leaves and seizing upon various insects.

Our Insect Musicians

When the monsoon with its magic touch brings life and greenness to rock and earth and withered tree, our insect musicians are roused to their greatest activity. The whole air at dusk seems to tinkle and murmur to their music. To the shrilling of the grasshoppers is added the staccato notes of the crickets, while in the grass myriads of lesser artistes provide a medley of sounds.

As musicians the cicadas are in a class of their own. There are many species of the cicada in India, most of them forest dwellers. All through the hot weather their screaming chorus rings through the forest, while a shower of rain, far from damping their ardour, only rouses them to a defeating crescendo of effort.

The ancient Greeks knew the cicada well. They called him tetix, and appreciated his music so much that they kept him captive in a cage to hear him sing. Well, there is no accounting for tastes!

Only the males were chosen—for the females, as with most insect musicians, are completely dumb. This moved one chauvinistic Greek poet to exclaim: 'Happy the cicadas, for they have voiceless wives!'

The music of the cicadas varies. Each species plays its distinctive tune. Their music-producing instruments are so complex that they must be regarded amongst the most remarkable sound-producing organs in the animal kingdom.

The underside of a cicada's body carries a pair of flaps, each of which covers an oval membrane which looks like the head of a drum, set in a solid rim of the body wall. The cicada does not beat his drums. They are set into intense vibration by a great pair of muscles attached to them from within the body. The sound is produced by the vibration of the drums, while the whole abdomen, which is practically hollow, helps to increase or diminish the sound, according to the position of the covering flaps. Simple, isn't it? To be truthful, I find it extremely complicated, and am able to describe the process only by consulting the notes of S.H. Prater, one-time curator of the Bombay Natural History Society.

Let it be added that the female carries these structures in a modified form, but, as she has no muscles to bring them into play, she is unable to use them. This is why she must remain silent while her spouse shrieks away. I would change the line from that Greek poet (Xenarchos, I think) and say instead: 'Pity the female cicadas, for they have singing husbands!'

Perhaps the most familiar and homely of insect singers are the crickets. I won't go into detail over how the cricket produces its music, except to say that its louder notes are produced by a rapid vibration of the wings, the right wing usually working over the left, the edge of one acting on the file of the other to produce a shrill, long-sustained note.

One of our best-known crickets is a large black fellow who lives underground and rarely comes out by day, except when the rains flood him out of his burrow. But when night falls, he sits on his doorstep and pours out his soul in a strident song. This cricket's name is as impressive as his sound—*Brachytrypes portentosus*.

The mole-cricket is a genius by itself. Mole-crickets are tillers of the soil. They use their powerful forelimbs for shovelling up the earth and their hard heads for butting into it. Notwithstanding its earthy occupations, the mole-cricket is sometimes moved to creating music. But as he repeats his note, a solemn deep-toned chirp, about a hundred times a minute, the performance can be monotonous.

In India, the cone-headed kattydids are probably the most notable performers. Kattydids are trim, slender grasshopper-like insects, much in evidence in the fresh green grass of the monsoon. In the fields the loud shrill notes of the males may be heard both by day and by night. Sometimes one of them comes into the house and treats its occupants to a sudden outburst of high-pitched fiddling. His song rises in pitch as the performer warms to his work. In a room it can be quite deafening; and the sound is always difficult to locate—it seems to come from everywhere.

Finally we come to the tree crickets, a band of willing artists who commence their performance at dusk. Their sounds are familiar, but it is difficult to see the musicians. Delicate pale green creatures with transparent green wings, they are hard to find among the foliage. And a tap on the bush or leaf on which they sit will put an immediate end to the performance.

Presumably the males sing in order to attract their more silent females. The music advertises the presence of the male, just as in other creatures it is colour or smell that does the job. After a performance, the female can sometimes be seen feeding off a sweet nectar that is contained in a cavity just behind the male's wings. Well, even the human male seeks to please his sweetheart with the offer of chocolates. And if music be the food of love, play on, cicada!

The Whistling Schoolboy

From the gorge above Gangotri
Down to Kochi by the sea,
The whistling-thrush keeps singing
His constant melody.

He was a whistling schoolboy once,
Who heard Lord Krishna's flute,
And tried to play the same sweet tune,
But struck a faulty note.

Said Krishna to the erring youth:
A bird you must become,
And you shall whistle all your days
Until your song is done.

IX

Big-cat Tales

'Why do you write so many stories about leopards?' asked a young reader.

'Because they are such fascinating creatures,' I said. 'Lithe, sinewy, powerful—beautiful, in fact.'

And I am glad to say that leopards are on the increase, although they do occasionally attack domestic animals. But the hills and forests are extensive enough for leopards to roam freely; they do their best to keep away from humans.

How can there be an India without leopards and tigers?

A Vision at Midnight

Sal trees near Rajpur. A lovely sight—varying shades of green; new leaf freshened by recent rain. And then, returning to Mussoorie around midnight, saw a leopard leap over the parapet wall, then her three cubs scurrying into the bushes. I thought I'd seen my last leopard some years ago, but in the hills this is obviously an animal that knows how to survive.

Romance Still Rides the Nine-Fifteen

I was at a wayside stop, on a line that went through the Terai forests near the foothills of the Himalayas. At about ten at night, the khilasi, or station watchman, lit his kerosene lamp and started walking up the track into the jungle. He was a Gujjar, and his true vocation was the keeping of buffaloes, but the breaking up of his tribe had led him into this strange new occupation.

'Where are you going?' I asked.

'To see if the tunnel is clear,' he said. 'The Mail train comes in twenty minutes.'

So I went with him, a furlong or two along the tracks, through a deep cutting which led to the tunnel. Every night, the khilasi walked through the dark tunnel, and then stood outside to wave his lamp to the oncoming train as a signal that the track was clear. If the engine driver did not see the lamp, he stopped the train. It always slowed down near the cutting. Having inspected the tunnel, we stood outside, waiting for the train. It seemed to take a long time in coming. There was no moon, and the dense forest seemed to be trying to crowd us into the narrow cutting. The sounds of the forest came to us on the night wind—the belling of a sambar, the cry of a fox, told us that perhaps a tiger or a leopard was on the prowl. There were strange nocturnal bird and insect sounds, and then silence.

The khilasi stood outside the tunnel, trimming his lamp, listening to the faint sounds of the jungle— sounds which only he, a Gujjar, who had grown up on the fringe of the forest, could identify and understand. Something made him stand very still for a few moments, peering into the darkness, and I could sense that everything was not as it should be.

'There is something in the tunnel,' he said.

I could hear nothing at first; but then there came a regular sawing sound, just like the sound of someone sawing through the branch of a tree.

'Baghera!' whispered the khilasi. He had said enough to enable me to recognize the sound—that of a leopard trying to find its mate.

I thought how fortunate we were that it had not been there when we walked through the tunnel. A leopard is unpredictable. But so is a khilasi.

'The train will be coming soon,' he whispered urgently, 'we must drive the animal out of the tunnel, or it will be killed.'

He must have sensed my astonishment, because he said, 'Do not worry, sahib. I know this leopard well. We have seen each other many times. He has a weakness for stray dogs and goats, but he will not harm us.'

He gave me his small handaxe to hold, and, raising his lamp high, started walking into the tunnel, shouting at the top of his voice to try and scare away the animal. I followed close behind him.

We had gone about twenty yards into the tunnel when the light from the khilasi's lamp fell on the leopard, who was crouching between the tracks, only about fifteen feet from us.

He was not a big leopard, but he was lithe and sinewy. Baring his teeth in a snarl, he went down on his belly, tail twitching, and I felt sure he was going to spring.

The khilasi and I both shouted together. Our voices rang and echoed through the tunnel. And the frightened leopard, uncertain of how many human beings were in there with him, turned swiftly and disappeared into the darkness.

As we returned to the tunnel entrance, the rails began to hum and we knew the train was coming.

I put my hand to one of the rails and felt its tremor. And then the engine came round the bend, hissing at us, scattering sparks into the darkness, defying the jungle as it roared through the steep sides of the cutting. It charged straight at the tunnel, and into it, thundering past us like some beautiful dragon from my childhood dreams. And when it had gone the silence returned, and the forest breathed again. Only the rails still trembled with the passing of the train.

As they tremble now to the passing of my own train, rushing through the night with its complement of precious humans, while somewhere at a lonely cutting in the foothills, a small thin man, who must always remain a firefly to these travelling thousands, lights up the darkness for steam engines and panthers.

And yet, for the khilasi himself, the incident I have recalled was not an adventure; it was a duty, a job of work, an everyday incident.

For me, all are significant: the lighted compartment with its farmers, shopkeepers, artisans, clerks and occasional pickpockets; and the lonely wayside stop, with its uncorrupted lamplighter.

Romance still rides the nine-fifteen.

Good Day to You, Uncle

On the left bank of the Ganga, where it emerges from the Himalayan foothills, there is a long stretch of heavy forest. There are villages on the fringe of the forest, inhabited by bamboo cutters and farmers, but there are few signs of commerce or pilgrimage. Hunters, however, have found the area an ideal hunting ground during the last seventy years, and as a result, the animals are not as numerous as they used to be. The trees, too, have been disappearing slowly; and, as the forest recedes, the animals lose their food and shelter and move further on into the foothills. Slowly, they are being denied the right to live.

Only the elephants can cross the river. And two years ago, when a large area of the forest was cleared to make way for a refugee resettlement camp, a herd of elephants—finding their favourite food, the green shoots of the bamboo, in short supply—waded across the river. They crashed through the suburbs of Hardwar, knocked down a factory wall, pulled down several tin roofs, held up a train, and left a trail of devastation in their wake until they found a new home in a new forest which was still untouched. Here, they settled down to a new life—but an unsettled, wary life. They did not know when men would appear again, with tractors, bulldozers and dynamite.

There was a time when the forest on the banks of the Ganga had provided food and shelter for some thirty or forty tigers; but men in search of trophies had shot them all, and now there remained only one old tiger in the jungle. Many hunters had tried to get him, but he was a wise and crafty old tiger, who knew the ways of men, and he had so far survived all attempts on his life.

Although the tiger had passed the prime of his life, he had lost none of his majesty. His muscles rippled beneath the golden yellow of his coat, and he walked through the long grass with the confidence of one who knew that he was still a king, even though his subjects were fewer. His great head pushed through the foliage, and it was only his tail, swinging high, that showed occasionally above the sea of grass.

Often he headed for water, the only water in the forest (if you don't count the river, which was several miles away), the water of a large jheel, which was almost a lake during the rainy season, but just a muddy marsh at this time of the year, in the late spring.

Here, at different times of the day and night, all the animals came to drink—the long-horned sambur, the delicate chital, the swamp deer, the hyaenas and jackals, the wild boar, the panthers—and the lone tiger. Since the elephants had gone, the water was usually clear except when buffaloes from the nearby village came to wallow in it. These buffaloes, though not wild, were not afraid of the panther or even of the tiger. They knew the panther was afraid of their massive horns and that the tiger preferred the flesh of the deer.

One day, there were several samburs at the water's edge; but they did not stay long. The scent of the tiger came with the breeze, and there was no mistaking its strong feline odour. The deer held their heads high for a few moments, their nostrils twitching, and then scattered into the forest, disappearing behind a screen of leaf and bamboo.

When the tiger arrived, there was no other animal near the water. But the birds were still there. The egrets continued to wade in the shallows, and a kingfisher darted low over the water, dived suddenly, a flash of blue and gold, and made off with a slim silver fish, which glistened in the sun like a polished gem. A long brown snake glided in and out among the waterlilies and disappeared beneath a fallen tree which lay rotting in the shallows.

The tiger waited in the shelter of a rock, his ears pricked up for the least unfamiliar sound, for he knew that it was at that place that men sometimes sat up for him with guns for they coveted his beauty—his stripes, and the gold of his body, his fine teeth, his whiskers, and his noble head. They would have liked to hang his skin on a wall, with his head stuffed and mounted, and pieces of glass replacing his fierce eyes; then they would have boasted of their triumph over the king of the jungle.

The tiger had been hunted before, so he did not usually show himself in the open during the day. But of late he had heard no guns, and if there were hunters around, you would have heard their guns (for a man with a gun cannot resist letting it off, even if it is only at a rabbit—or at another man). And, besides, the tiger was thirsty.

He was also feeling quite hot. It was March and the shimmering dust haze of summer had come early. Tigers—unlike other cats—are fond of water, and on a hot day will wallow in it for hours.

He walked into the water, in amongst the water lilies, and drank slowly. He was seldom in a hurry when he ate or drank. Other animals might bolt down their food, but they were only other animals. A tiger is a tiger; he has his dignity to preserve even though he isn't aware of it!

He raised his head and listened, one paw suspended in the air. A strange sound had come to him with the breeze, and he was wary of strange sounds. So he moved swiftly into the shelter of the tall grass that bordered the jheel, and climbed a hillock until he reached his favourite rock. This rock was big enough both to hide him and to give him shade. Anyone looking up from the jheel might think it strange that the rock had a round bump on the top. The bump was the tiger's head. He kept it very still.

The sound he heard was only the sound of a flute, rendered thin and reedy in the forest. It belonged to Ramu, a slim brown boy who rode a buffalo. Ramu played vigorously on the flute. Shyam, a slightly smaller boy, riding another buffalo, brought up the rear of the herd.

There were about eight buffaloes in the herd, and they belonged to the families of the two friends Ramu and Shyam. Their people were Gujjars, a nomadic community who earned a livelihood by keeping buffaloes and selling milk and butter. The boys were about twelve years old, but they could not have told you exactly because in their village nobody thought birthdays were important. They were almost the same age as the tiger, but he was old and experienced while they were still cubs.

The tiger had often seen them at the tank, and he was not worried by their presence. He knew the village people would do him no harm as long as he left their buffaloes alone. Once when he was younger and full of bravado, he had killed a buffalo—not because he was hungry, but because he was young and wanted to try out his strength—and after that the villagers had hunted him for days, with spears, bows and an old muzzle loader. Now he left the buffaloes alone, even though the deer in the forest were not as numerous as before.

The boys knew that a tiger lived in the jungle, for they had often heard him roar; but they did not suspect that he was so near just then.

The tiger gazed down from his rock, and the sight of eight fat black buffaloes made him give a low, throaty moan. But, the boys were there, and, besides, a buffalo was not easy to kill.

He decided to move on and find a cool shady place in the heart of the jungle, where he could rest during the warm afternoon and be free of the flies and mosquitoes that swarmed around the jheel. At night he would hunt.

With a lazy, half-humorous roar—'a-oonh!'—he got up off his haunches and sauntered off into the jungle.

Even the gentlest of the tiger's roars can be heard half a mile away, and the boys who were barely fifty yards away, looked up immediately.

'There he goes!' said Ramu, taking the flute from his lips and pointing it towards the hillocks. He was not afraid, for he knew that this tiger was not interested in humans. 'Did you see him?'

'I saw his tail, just before he disappeared. He's a big tiger!'

'Do not call him tiger. Call him Uncle, or Maharaj.'

'Oh, why?'

'Don't you know that it's unlucky to call a tiger a tiger? My father always told me so. But if you meet a tiger and call him Uncle, he will leave you alone.'

'I'll try and remember that,' said Shyam.

The buffaloes were now well inside the water, and some of them were lying down in the mud. Buffaloes love soft wet mud and will wallow in it for hours. The slushier the mud the better. Ramu, to avoid being dragged down into the mud with his buffalo, slipped off its back and plunged into the water. He waded to a small islet covered with reeds and water lilies. Shyam was close behind him.

They lay down on their hard flat stomachs, on a patch of grass, and allowed the warm sun to beat down on their bare brown bodies.

Ramu was the more knowledgeable boy, because he had been to Hardwar and Dehra Dun several times with his father. Shyam had never been out of the village.

Shyam said, 'The jheel is not so deep this year.'

'We have had no rain since January,' said Ramu. 'If we do not get rain soon the jheel may dry up altogether.'

'And then what will we do?'

'We? I don't know. There is a well in the village. But even that may dry up. My father told me that it failed once, just about the time I was born, and everyone had to walk ten miles to the river for water.'

'And what about the animals?'

'Some will stay here and die. Others will go to the river. But there are too many people near the river now—and temples, houses and factories—and the animals stay away. And the trees have been cut, so that between the jungle and the river there is no place to hide. Animals are afraid of the open—they are afraid of men with guns.'

'Even at night?'

'At night men come in jeeps, with searchlights. They kill the deer for meat, and sell the skins of tigers and panthers.'

'I didn't know a tiger's skin was worth anything.'

'It's worth more than our skins,' said Ramu knowingly. 'It will fetch six hundred rupees. Who would pay that much for one of us?'

'Our fathers would.'

'True, if they had the money.'

'If my father sold his fields, he would get more than six hundred rupees.'

'True, but if he sold his fields, none of you would have anything to eat. A man needs the land as much as a tiger needs the jungle.'

'Yes,' said Shyam. 'And that reminds me—my mother asked me to take some roots home.'

'I will help you.'

They walked deeper into the jheel until the water was up to their waists, and began pulling up water lilies by the roots. The flower is beautiful but the villagers value the root more. When it is cooked, it makes a delicious and strengthening dish. The plant multiplies rapidly and is always in good supply. In the year when famine hit the village, it was only the root of the water lily that saved many from starvation.

When Shyam and Ramu had finished gathering roots, they emerged from the water and passed the time in wrestling with each other, slipping about in the soft mud which soon covered them from head to toe.

To get rid of the mud, they dived into the water again and swam across to their buffaloes. Then, jumping on their backs and digging their heels into thick hides, the boys raced them across the jheel, shouting and hollering so much that all the birds flew away in fright, and the monkeys set up a shrill chattering of their own in the dhak trees.

It was evening, and the twilight fading fast, when the buffalo herd finally wended its way homeward, to be greeted outside the village by the barking of dogs, the gurgle of hookah pipes, and the homely smell of cow-dung smoke.

The tiger made a kill that night—a chital. He made his approach against the wind so that the unsuspecting spotted deer did not see him until it was too late. A blow on the deer's haunches from the tiger's paw brought it down, and then the great beast fastened his fangs on the deer's throat. It was all over in a few minutes. The tiger was too quick and strong, and the deer did not struggle much.

It was a violent end for so gentle a creature. But you must not imagine that in the jungle the deer live in permanent fear of death. It is only man, with his imagination and his fear of the hereafter, who is afraid of dying. In the jungle it is different. Sudden death appears at intervals. Wild creatures do not have to think about it, and so the sudden killing of one of their number by some predator of the forest is only a fleeting incident, soon forgotten by the survivors.

The tiger feasted well, growling with pleasure as he ate his way up the body, leaving the entrails. When he had his night's fill he left the carcase for the vultures and jackals. The cunning old tiger never returned to the same carcase, even if there was still plenty left to eat. In the past, when he had gone back to a kill he had often found a man sitting in a tree waiting for him with a rifle.

His belly filled, the tiger sauntered over to the edge of the forest and looked out across the sandy wasteland and the deep, singing river, at the twinkling lights of Rishikesh on the opposite bank, and raised his head and roared his defiance at mankind.

He was a lonesome bachelor. It was five or six years since he had a mate. She had been shot by the trophy hunters, and her two cubs had been trapped by men who do trade in wild animals. One went to a circus, where he had to learn tricks to amuse people and respond to the flick of a whip; the other, more fortunate, went first to a zoo in Delhi and was later transferred to a zoo in America.

Sometimes, when the old tiger was very lonely, he gave a great roar, which could be heard throughout the forest. The villagers thought he was roaring in anger, but the jungle knew that he was really roaring out of loneliness.

When the sound of his roar had died away, he paused, standing still, waiting for an answering roar; but it never came. It was taken up instead by the shrill scream of a barbet high up in a sal tree.

It was dawn now, dew-fresh and cool, and jungle dwellers were on the move . . .

The black beady little eyes of a jungle rat were fixed on a small brown hen who was pecking around in the undergrowth near her nest. He had a large family to feed, this rat, and he knew that in the hen's nest was a clutch of delicious fawn-coloured eggs. He waited patiently for nearly an hour before he had the satisfaction of seeing the hen leave her nest and go off in search of food.

As soon as she had gone, the rat lost no time in making his raid. Slipping quietly out of his hole, he slithered along among the leaves; but, clever as he was, he did not realize that his own movements were being watched.

A pair of grey mongooses scouted about in the dry grass. They too were hungry, and eggs usually figured in large measure on their menu. Now, lying still on an outcrop of rock, they watched the rat sneaking along, occasionally sniffing at the air and finally vanishing behind a boulder. When he reappeared, he was struggling to roll an egg uphill towards his hole.

The rat was in difficulty, pushing the egg sometimes with his paws, sometimes with his nose. The ground was rough, and the egg wouldn't move straight. Deciding that he must have help, he scuttled off to call his spouse. Even now the mongooses did not descend on that tantalizing egg. They waited until the rat returned with his wife, and then watched as the male rat took the egg firmly between his forepaws and rolled over on to his back. The female rat then grabbed her mate's tail and began to drag him along.

Totally absorbed in their struggle with the egg, the rat did not hear the approach of the mongooses. When these two large furry visitors suddenly bobbed up from behind a stone, the rats squealed with fright, abandoned the egg, and fled for their lives.

The mongooses wasted no time in breaking open the egg and making a meal of it. But just as, a few minutes ago, the rat had not noticed their approach, so now they too did not notice the village boy, carrying a small bright axe and a net bag in his hands, creeping along.

Ramu too was searching for eggs, and when he saw the mongooses busy with one, he stood still to watch them, his eyes roving in search of the nest. He was hoping the mongooses would lead him to the nest; but, when they had finished their meal and made off into the undergrowth, Ramu had to do his own searching. He failed to find the nest, and moved further into the forest. The rat's hopes were just reviving when, to his disgust, the mother hen returned.

Ramu now made his way to a mahua tree.

The flowers of the mahua can be eaten by animals as well as by men. Bears are particularly fond of them and will eat large quantities of flowers which gradually start fermenting in their stomachs with the result that the animals get quite drunk. Ramu had often seen a couple of bears stumbling home to their cave, bumping into each other or into the trunks of trees. They are short-sighted to begin with, and when drunk can hardly see at all. But their sense of smell and hearing are so good that in the end they find their way home.

Ramu decided he would gather some mahua flowers, and climbed up the tree, which is leafless when it blossoms. He began breaking the white flowers and throwing them to the ground. He had been on the tree for about five minutes when he heard the whining grumble of a bear, and presently a young sloth bear ambled into the clearing beneath the tree.

He was a small bear, little more than a cub, and Ramu was not frightened; but, because he thought the mother might be in the vicinity, he decided to take no chance, and sat very still, waiting to see what the bear would do. He hoped it wouldn't choose the mahua tree for a meal.

At first the young bear put his nose to the ground and sniffed his way along until he came to a large anthill. Here he began huffing and puffing, blowing rapidly in and out of his nostrils, causing the dust from the anthill to fly in all directions. But he was disappointed because the anthill had been deserted long ago. And so, grumbling, he made his way across to a tall wild-plum tree, and, shinning rapidly up the smooth trunk, was soon perched on its topmost branches. It was only then that he saw Ramu.

The bear at once scrambled several feet higher up the tree, and laid himself out flat on a branch. It wasn't a very thick branch and left a large part of the bear's body showing on either side. The bear tucked his head away behind another branch, and so long as he could not see Ramu, seemed quite satisfied that he was well hidden, though he couldn't help grumbling with anxiety, for a bear, like most animals, is afraid of man.

Bears, however, are also very curious, and curiosity has often led them into trouble. Slowly, inch by inch, the young bear's black snout appeared over the edge of the branch; but immediately as the eyes came into view and met Ramu's, he drew back with a jerk and the head was once more hidden. The bear did this two or three times, and Ramu, highly amused, waited until it wasn't looking, then moved some way down the tree. When the bear looked up again and saw that the boy was missing, he was so pleased with himself that he stretched right across to the next branch, to get a plum. Ramu chose this moment to burst into loud laughter. The startled bear tumbled out of the tree, dropped through the branches for a distance of some fifteen feet, and landed with a thud in a heap of dry leaves.

And then several things happened at almost the same time.

The mother bear came charging into the clearing. Spotting Ramu in the tree, she reared up on her hind legs, grunting fiercely. It was Ramu's turn to be startled. There are few animals more dangerous than a rampaging mother bear, and the boy knew that one blow from her clawed forepaws could rip his skull open.

But before the bear could approach the tree, there was a tremendous roar, and the old tiger bounded into the clearing. He had been asleep in the bushes not far away—he liked a good sleep after a heavy meal—and the noise in the clearing had woken him.

He was in a bad mood, and his loud 'a-oonh!' made his displeasure quite clear. The bear turned and ran from the clearing, the youngster squealing with fright.

The tiger then came into the centre of the clearing, looked up at the trembling boy, and roared again.

Ramu nearly fell out of the tree.

'Good day to you, Uncle,' he stammered, showing his teeth in a nervous grin.

Perhaps this was too much for the tiger. With a low growl, he turned his back on the mahua tree and padded off into the jungle, his tail twitching in disgust.

That night, when Ramu told his parents and his grandfather about the tiger and how it had saved him from a female bear, it started a round of tiger stories—about how some of them could be gentlemen, others rogues. Sooner or later the conversation came round to man-eaters, and Grandfather told two stories which he swore were true, although his listeners only half-believed him.

The first story concerned the belief that a man-eating tiger is guided towards his next victim by the spirit of a human being previously killed and eaten by the tiger. Grandfather said that he actually knew three hunters, who sat up in a *machan* over a human kill, and that, when the tiger came, the corpse sat up and pointed with his right hand at the men in the tree. The tiger then went away. But the hunters knew he would return, and one man was brave enough to get down from the tree and tie the right arm of the corpse to its side. Later, when the tiger returned, the corpse sat up, and this time pointed out the men with his left hand. The enraged tiger sprang into the tree and killed his enemies in the machan.

'And then there was a *bania*,' said Grandfather, beginning another story, 'who lived in a village in the jungle. He wanted to visit a neighbouring village to collect some money that was owed to him, but as the road lay through heavy forest in which lived a terrible man-eating tiger, he did not know what to do. Finally, he went to a sadhu who gave him two powders. By eating the first powder, he could turn into a huge tiger, capable of dealing with any other tiger in the jungle, and by eating the second he could become a bania again.

'Armed with his two powders, and accompanied by his pretty young wife, the bania set out on his journey. They had not gone far into the forest when they came upon the man-eater sitting in the middle of the road. Before swallowing the first powder, the bania told his wife to stay where she was, so that when he returned after killing the tiger, she could at once give him the second powder and enable him to resume his old shape.

'Well, the bania's plan worked, but only up to a point. He swallowed the first powder and immediately became a magnificent tiger. With a great roar, he bounded towards the man-eater, and after a brief, furious fight, killed his opponent.

Then, with his jaws still dripping blood, he returned to his wife.

'The poor girl was terrified and spilt the second powder on the ground. The bania was so angry that he pounced on his wife and killed and ate her. And afterwards this terrible tiger was so enraged at not being able to become a human again that he killed and ate hundreds of people all over the country.'

'The only people he spared,' added Grandfather, with a twinkle in his eyes, 'were those who owed him money. A bania never gives up a loan as lost, and the tiger still hoped that one day he might become a human again and be able to collect his dues.'

Next morning, when Ramu came back from the well, which was used to irrigate his father's fields, he found a crowd of curious children surrounding a jeep and three strangers. Each of the strangers had a gun, and they were accompanied by two bearers and a vast amount of provisions.

They had heard that there was a tiger in the area, and they wanted to shoot it.

One of the hunters, who looked even more strange than the others, had come all the way from America to shoot a tiger, and he vowed that he would not leave the country without a tiger's skin in his baggage. One of his companions had said that he could buy a tiger's skin in Delhi, but the hunter said he preferred to get his own trophies.

These men had money to spend, and, as most of the villagers needed money badly, they were only too willing to go into the forest to construct a machan for the hunters. The platform, big enough to take the three men, was put up in the branches of a tall tun, or mahogany tree.

It was the only night the hunters used the machan. At the end of March, though the days are warm, the nights are still cold. The hunters had neglected to bring blankets, and by midnight their teeth were chattering. Ramu, having tied up a buffalo calf for them at the foot of the tree, made as if to go home but instead circled the area, hanging up bits and pieces of old clothing on small trees and bushes. He thought he owed that much to the tiger. He knew the wily old king of the jungle would keep well away from the bait if he saw the bits of clothing—for where there were men's clothes, there would be men.

The vigil lasted well into the night but the tiger did not come near the tun tree, perhaps he wasn't hungry, perhaps he got Ramu's message. In any case, the men in the tree soon gave themselves away.

The cold was really too much for them. A flask of rum was produced, and passed around, and it was not long before there was more purpose to finishing the rum than to finishing off a tiger. Silent at first, the men soon began talking in whispers; and to jungle creatures a human whisper is as telling as a trumpet call.

Soon the men were quite merry, talking in loud voices. And when the first morning light crept over the forest, and Ramu and his friends came back to fetch the great hunters, they found them fast asleep in the machan.

The hunters looked surly and embarrassed as they trudged back to the village.

'No game left in these parts,' said the American.

'Wrong time of the year for tiger,' said the second man.

'Don't know what the country's coming to,' said the third.

And complaining about the weather, the poor quality of cartridges, the quantity of rum they had drunk, and the perversity of tigers, they drove away in disgust.

It was not until the onset of summer that an event occurred which altered the hunting habits of the old tiger and brought him into conflict with the villagers.

There had been no rain for almost two months, and the tall jungle grass had become a sea of billowy dry yellow. Some refugee settlers, living in an area where the forest had been cleared, had been careless while cooking and had started a jungle fire. Slowly it spread into the interior, from where the acrid smell and the fumes smoked the tiger out toward the edge of the jungle. As night came on, the flames grew more vivid, and the smell stronger. The tiger turned and made for the jheel, where he knew he would be safe, provided he swam across to the little island in the centre.

Next morning he was on the island, which was untouched by the fire. But his surroundings had changed. The slopes of the hills were black with burnt grass, and most of the tall bamboo had disappeared. The deer and the wild pig, finding that their natural cover had gone, fled further east.

When the fire had died down and the smoke had cleared, the tiger prowled through the forest again but found no game. Once he came across the body of a burnt rabbit, but he could not eat it. He drank at the jheel and settled down in a shady spot to sleep the day away. Perhaps, by evening, some of the animals would return; if not, he too would have to look for new hunting grounds—or new game.

The tiger spent five more days looking for a suitable game to kill. By that time he was so hungry that he even resorted to rooting among the dead leaves and burnt out stumps of trees, searching for worms and beetles. This was a sad come-down for the king of the jungle. But even now he hesitated to leave the area, for he had a deep suspicion and fear of the forests further east—forests that were fast being swallowed up by human habitation. He could have gone north, into high mountains, but they did not provide him with the long grass he needed. A panther could manage quite well up there, but not a tiger who loved the natural privacy of the heavy jungle. In the hills, he would have to hide all the time.

At break of day, the tiger came to the jheel. The water was now shallow and muddy, and a green scum had spread over the top. But it was still drinkable and the tiger quenched his thirst.

He lay down across his favourite rock, hoping for a deer but none came. He was about to get up and go away when he heard an animal approach.

The tiger at once leaped off his perch and flattened himself on the ground, his tawny striped skin merging with the dry grass. A heavy animal was moving through the bushes, and the tiger waited patiently.

A buffalo emerged and came to the water.

The buffalo was alone.

He was a big male, and his long curved horns lay right back across his shoulders. He moved leisurely towards the water, completely unaware of the tiger's presence.

The tiger hesitated before making his charge. It was a long time—many years—since he had killed a buffalo, and he knew the villagers would not like it. But the pangs of hunger overcame his scruples. There was no morning breeze, everything was still, and the smell of the tiger did not reach the buffalo. A monkey chattered on a nearby tree, but his warning went unheeded.

Crawling stealthily on his stomach, the tiger skirted the edge of the jheel and approached the buffalo from the rear. The water birds, who were used to the presence of both animals, did not raise an alarm.

Getting closer, the tiger glanced around to see if there were men, or other buffaloes, in the vicinity. Then, satisfied that he was alone, he crept forward. The buffalo was drinking, standing in shallow water at the edge of the tank, when the tiger charged from the side and bit deep into the animal's thigh.

The buffalo turned to fight, but the tendons of his right hind leg had been snapped, and he could only stagger forward a few paces. But he was a buffalo—the bravest of the domestic cattle. He was not afraid. He snorted, and lowered his horns at the tiger; but the great cat was too fast, and circling the buffalo, bit into the other hind leg.

The buffalo crashed to the ground, both hind legs crippled, and then the tiger dashed in, using both tooth and claw, biting deep into the buffalo's throat until blood gushed out from the jugular vein.

The buffalo gave one long, last bellow before dying.

The tiger, having rested, now began to gorge himself, but, even though he had been starving for days, he could not finish the huge carcase. At least one good meal still remained, when, satisfied and feeling his strength returning, he quenched his thirst at the jheel. Then he dragged the remains of the buffalo into the bushes to hide it from the vultures, and went off to find a place to sleep.

He would return to the kill when he was hungry again.

The villagers were upset when they discovered that a buffalo was missing; and next day, when Ramu and Shyam came running home to say that they found the carcase near the jheel, half eaten by a tiger, the men were disturbed and angry. They felt that the tiger had tricked and deceived them. And they knew that once he got a taste for domestic cattle he would make a habit of slaughtering them.

Kundan Singh, Shyam's father and the owner of the dead buffalo, said he would go after the tiger himself.

'It is all very well to talk about what you will do to the tiger,' said his wife, 'but you should never have let the buffalo go off on its own.'

'He had been out on his own before,' said Kundan. 'This is the first time the tiger has attacked one of our beasts. A devil must have entered the Maharaj.'

'He must have been very hungry,' said Shyam.

'Well, we are hungry too,' said Kundan Singh.

'Our best buffalo—the only male in our herd.'

'The tiger will kill again,' said Ramu's father.

'If we let him,' said Kundan.

'Should we send for the shikaris?'

'No. They were not clever. The tiger will escape them easily. Besides, there is no time. The tiger will return for another meal tonight. We must finish him off ourselves!'

'But how?'

Kundan Singh smiled secretively, played with the ends of his moustache for a few moments, and then, with great pride, produced from under his cot a double-barrelled gun of ancient vintage.

'My father bought it from an Englishman,' he said.

'How long ago was that?'

'At the time I was born.'

'And have you ever used it?' asked Ramu's father, who was not sure that the gun would work.

'Well, some years back, I let it off at some bandits. You remember the time when those dacoits raided our village? They chose the wrong village, and were severely beaten for their pains. As they left, I fired my gun off at them. They didn't stop running until they crossed the Ganga!'

'Yes, but did you hit anyone?'

'I would have, if someone's goat hadn't got in the way at the last moment. But we had roast mutton that night! Don't worry, brother, I know how the thing fires.'

Accompanied by Ramu's father and some others, Kundan set out for the jheel, where, without shifting the buffalo's carcase—for they knew that the tiger would not come near them if he suspected a trap—they made another machan in the branches of a tall tree some thirty feet from the kill.

Later that evening, Kundan Singh and Ramu's father settled down for the night on their crude platform on the tree.

Several hours passed, and nothing but a jackal was seen by the watchers. And then, just as the moon came up over the distant hills, Kundan and his companion were startled by a low 'A-ooonh', followed by a suppressed, rumbling growl.

Kundan grasped his old gun, whilst his friend drew closer to him for comfort. There was complete silence for a minute or two—time that was an agony of suspense for the watchers—and then the sound of stealthy footfalls on dead leaves under the trees.

A moment later the tiger walked out into the moonlight and stood over his kill.

At first Kundan could do nothing. He was completely overawed by the size of this magnificent tiger. Ramu's father had to nudge him, and then Kundan quickly put the gun to his shoulder, aimed at the tiger's head, and pressed the trigger.

The gun went off with a flash and two loud bangs as Kundan fired both barrels. Then there was a tremendous roar. One of the bullets had grazed the tiger's head.

The enraged animal rushed at the tree and tried to leap on to the branches. Fortunately, the machan had been built at a safe height, and the tiger was unable to reach it. It roared again and then bounded off into the forest.

'What a tiger!' exclaimed Kundan, half in fear and half in admiration. 'I feel as though my liver has turned to water.'

'You missed him completely,' said Ramu's father. 'Your gun makes big noise; an arrow would have done more damage.'

'I did not miss him,' said Kundan, feeling offended. 'You heard him roar, didn't you? Would he have been so angry had he not been hit? If I have wounded him badly, he will die.'

'And if you have wounded him slightly, he may turn into a man-eater, and then where will we be?'

'I don't think he will come back,' said Kundan. 'He will leave these forests.'

They waited until the sun was up before coming down from the tree. They found a few drops of blood on the dry grass but no trail led into the forest, and Ramu's father was convinced that the wound was only a slight one.

The bullet, missing the fatal spot behind the ear, had only grazed the back of the skull and cut a deep groove at its base. It took a few days to heal, and during this time the tiger lay low and did not go near the jheel except when it was very dark and he was very thirsty.

The villagers thought the tiger had gone away,

and Ramu and Shyam—accompanied by some other youths, and always carrying axes and lathis—began bringing buffaloes to the tank again during the day; but they were careful not to let any of them stray far from the herd, and they returned home while it was still daylight.

It was some days since the jungle had been ravaged by the fire, and in the tropics the damage is repaired quickly. In spite of it being the dry season, new life soon began to creep into the forest.

While the buffaloes wallowed in the muddy water, and the boys wrestled on the grassy islet, a big tawny eagle soared high above them, looking for a meal—a sure sign that some of the animals were beginning to return to the forest. It was not long before his keen eyes detected a movement in the glade below.

What the eagle with his powerful eyesight saw was a baby hare, a small fluffy thing, its long pink-tinted ears laid flat along its sides. Had it not been creeping along between two large stones, it would have escaped notice. The eagle waited to see if the mother was about, and as he waited he realized that he was not the only one who coveted this juicy morsel. From the bushes there had appeared a sinuous yellow creature, pressed low to the ground and moving rapidly towards the hare. It was a yellow jungle cat, hardly noticeable in the scorched grass. With great stealth the jungle cat began to stalk the baby hare.

He pounced. The hare's squeal was cut short by the cat's cruel claws; but it had been heard by the mother hare, who now bounded into the glade and without the slightest hesitation went for the surprised cat.

There was nothing haphazard about the mother hare's attack. She flashed around behind the cat and jumped clean over it. As she landed, she kicked back, sending a stinging jet of dust shooting into the cat's face. She did this again and again.

The bewildered cat, crouching and snarling, picked up the kill and tried to run away with it. But the hare would not permit this. She continued her leaping and buffeting, till eventually the cat, out of sheer frustration, dropped the kill and attacked the mother.

The cat sprung at the hare a score of times, lashing out with his claws; but the mother hare was both clever and agile enough to keep just out of reach of those terrible claws, and drew the cat further and further away from her baby—for she did not as yet know that it was dead.

The tawny eagle saw his chance. Swift and true, he swooped. For a brief moment, as his wings overspread the puny little hare and his talons sank deep into it, he caught a glimpse of the cat racing towards him and the mother hare fleeing into the bushes. And then with a shrill 'kee-e e-ee' of triumph, he rose and whirled away with his dinner.

The boys had heard his shrill cry and looked up just in time to see the eagle flying over the jheel with the small little hare held firmly in its talons.

'Poor hare,' said Shyam. 'Its life was short.'

'That's the law of the jungle,' said Ramu. 'The eagle has a family too, and must feed it.'

'I wonder if we are any better than animals,' said Shyam.

'Perhaps we are a little better, in some ways,' said Ramu. 'Grandfather always says, "To be able to laugh and to be merciful are the only things that make man better than the beast."'

The next day, while the boys were taking the herd home, one of the buffaloes lagged behind. Ramu did not realize that the animal was missing until he heard an agonized bellow behind him. He glanced over his shoulder just in time to see the big striped tiger dragging the buffalo into a clump of young bamboo trees. At the same time the herd became aware of the danger and the buffaloes snorted with fear as they hurried along the forest path. To urge them forward, and to warn his friends, Ramu cupped his hands to his mouth and gave vent to a yodelling call.

The buffaloes bellowed, the boys shouted, and the birds flew shrieking from the trees. It was almost a stampede by the time the herd emerged from the forest. The villagers heard the thunder of hoofs, and saw the herd coming home amidst clouds of dust and confusion, and knew that something was wrong.

'The tiger!' shouted Ramu. 'He is here! He has killed one of the buffaloes.'

'He is afraid of us no longer,' said Shyam.

'Did you see where he went?' asked Kundan Singh, hurrying up to them.

'I remember the place,' said Ramu. 'He dragged the buffalo in amongst the bamboo.'

'Then there is no time to lose,' said his father. 'Kundan, you take your gun and two men, and wait near the suspension bridge, where the Garur stream joins the Ganga. The jungle is narrow there. We will beat the jungle from our side, and drive the tiger towards you. He will not escape us, unless he swims the river!'

'Good!' said Kundan, running into his house for his gun, with Shyam close at his heels. 'Was it one of our buffaloes again?' he asked.

'It was Ramu's buffalo this time,' said Shyam. 'A good milk buffalo.'

'Then Ramu's father will beat the jungle thoroughly. You boys had better come with me. It will not be safe for you to accompany the beaters.'

Kundan Singh, carrying his gun and accompanied by Ramu, Shyam and two men, headed for the river junction, while Ramu's father collected about twenty men from the village and, guided by one of the boys who had been with Ramu, made for the spot where the tiger had killed the buffalo.

The tiger was still eating when he heard the men coming. He had not expected to be disturbed so soon. With an angry 'whoof!' he bounded into a bamboo thicket and watched the men through a screen of leaves and tall grass.

The men did not seem to take much notice of the dead buffalo, but gathered round their leader and held a consultation. Most of them carried hand drums slung from their shoulders. They also carried sticks, spears and axes.

After a hurried conversation, they entered the denser part of the jungle, beating their drums with the palms of their hands. Some of the men banged empty kerosene tins. These made even more noise than the drums.

The tiger did not like the noise and retreated deeper into the jungle. But he was surprised to find that the men, instead of going away, came after him into the jungle, banging away on their drums and tins, and shouting at the top of their voices. They had separated now, and advanced single or in pairs, but nowhere were they more than fifteen yards apart. The tiger could easily have broken through this slowly advancing semicircle of men—one swift blow from his paw would have felled the strongest of them—but his main aim was to get away from the noise. He hated and feared noises made by men.

He was not a man-eater and he would not attack a man unless he was very angry or frightened

or very desperate; and he was none of these as yet.
He had eaten well, and he would have liked to rest
in peace—but there would be no rest for any animal
until the men ceased their tremendous clatter and
din.

For an hour Ramu's father and others beat the
jungle, calling, drumming and trampling the
undergrowth. The tiger had no rest. Whenever he
was able to put some distance between himself and
the men, he would sink down in some shady spot to
rest; but, within five or ten minutes, the trampling
and drumming would sound nearer, and the tiger,
with an angry snarl, would get up and pad north,
pad silently north along the narrowing strip of the
jungle, towards the junction of the Garur stream
and the Ganga. Ten years back, he would have had
the jungle on his right in which to hide; but the trees
had been felled long ago, to make way for humans
and houses, and now he could only move to the left,
towards the river.

It was after a long time that the tiger finally
appeared in the open. He longed for the darkness
and security of the night, for the sun was his enemy.
Kundan and the boys had a clear view of him as he
stalked slowly along, now in the open with the sun
glinting on his glossy side, now in the shade or
passing through the shorter reeds. He was still out
of range of Kundan's gun, but there was no fear of
his getting out of the beat, as the 'stops' were all

picked men from the village. He disappeared among some bushes but soon reappeared to retrace his steps, the beaters having done their work well. He was now only one hundred and fifty yards from the rocks where Kundan Singh waited, and he looked very big.

The beat had closed in, and the exit along the bank downstream was completely blocked, so the tiger turned into a belt of reeds, and Kundan Singh expected that the head would soon peer out of the cover a few yards away. The beaters were now making a great noise, shouting and beating their drums, but nothing moved; and Ramu, watching from a distance, wondered, 'Has he slipped through the beaters?' And he half hoped so.

Tins clashed, drums beat, and some of the men poked into the reeds with their spears or long bamboos. Perhaps one of these thrusts found a mark, because at last the tiger was roused, and with an angry desperate snarl he charged out of the reeds, splashing his way through an inlet of mud and water.

Kundan Singh fired, and his bullet struck the tiger on the thigh.

The mighty animal stumbled; but he was up in a minute, and rushing through a gap in the narrowing line of beaters, he made straight for the only way across the river—the suspension bridge that passed over the Ganga here, providing a route into the high hills beyond.

We'll get him now,' said Kundan, priming his gun again. 'He's right in the open!'

The suspension bridge swayed and trembled as the wounded tiger lurched across it. Kundan fired, and this time the bullet grazed the tiger's shoulder. The animal bounded forward, lost his footing on the unfamiliar, slippery planks of the swaying bridge, and went over the side, falling headlong into the strong, swirling waters of the river.

He rose to the surface once, but the current took him under and away, and only a thin streak of blood remained on the river's surface.

Kundan and others hurried downstream to see if the dead tiger had been washed up on the river's banks; but though they searched the riverside several miles, they could not find the king of the forest.

He had not provided anyone with a trophy. His skin would not be spread on a couch, nor would his head be hung up on a wall. No claw of his would be hung as a charm around the neck of a child. No villager would use his fat as a cure for rheumatism.

At first the villagers were glad because they felt their buffaloes were safe. Then the men began to feel that something had gone out of their lives, out of the life of the forest; they began to feel that the forest was no longer a forest. It had been shrinking year by year, but, as long as the tiger had been there and the villagers had heard it roar at night, they had known that they were still secure from the intruders and newcomers who came to fell the trees and eat up the land and let the flood waters into the village. But, now that the tiger had gone, it was as though a protector had gone, leaving the forest open and vulnerable, easily destroyable. And, once the forest was destroyed, they too would be in danger.

There was another thing that had gone with the tiger, another thing that had been lost, a thing that was being lost everywhere—something called 'nobility'.

Ramu remembered something that his grandfather had once said, 'The tiger is the very soul of India, and when the last tiger has gone, so will the soul of the country.'

The boys lay flat on their stomachs on the little mud island and watched the monsoon clouds, gathering overhead.

'The king of our forest is dead,' said Shyam.'There are no more tigers.'

'There must be tigers,' said Ramu. 'How can there be an India without tigers?'

The river had carried the tiger many miles away from its home, from the forest it had always known, and brought it ashore on a strip of warm yellow sand, where it lay in the sun, quite still, but breathing.

Vultures gathered and waited at a distance, some of them perching on the branches of nearby trees.

But the tiger was more drowned than hurt, and

as the river water oozed out of his mouth, and the warm sun made new life throb through his body, he stirred and stretched, and his glazed eyes came into focus. Raising his head, he saw trees and tall grass.

Slowly he heaved himself off the ground and moved at a crouch to where the grass waved in the afternoon breeze. Would he be harried again, and shot at? There was no smell of Man. The tiger moved forward with greater confidence.

There was, however, another smell in the air—a smell that reached back to the time when he was young and fresh and full of vigour—a smell that he had almost forgotten but could never quite forget—the smell of a tigress!

He raised his head high, and new life surged through his tired limbs. He gave a full-throated roar and moved purposefully through the tall grass. And the roar came back to him, calling him, calling him forward—a roar that meant there would be more tigers in this land!

May There Always Be Tigers

May there always be tigers.
In the jungles and tall grass.
May the tiger's roar be heard,
May his thunder

Be known in the land.
At the forest pool, by moonlight
May he drink and raise his head
Scenting the night wind.
May he crouch low in the grass
When the herdsmen pass,
And slumber in dark caverns
When the sun is high.
May there always be tigers.
But not so many, that one of them
Might be tempted to come into my room
In search of a meal!

X
Nature's Fury

The relentless fury of a storm at sea was best captured by Conrad in his short story 'Typhoon'. When the pent-up forces of nature are released, there is little that humans can do about it, except try to survive.

Earthquake, tidal wave, hurricane, flood, blizzard, all come to remind us that we are not, after all, the masters of the universe. We might trample upon our natural heritage, and do our best to destroy it, but the forces of nature are greater than man's. Nature will always have the last word.

Earthquake in Assam

'If ever there's a calamity,' Grandmother used to say, 'it will find Grandfather in his bath.' Grandfather loved his bath, which he took in a large round aluminium tub, and sometimes spent as long as an hour in it, 'wallowing', as he called it, and splashing around like a boy.

He was in his bath during the earthquake that convulsed Bengal and Assam on 12 June 1897—an earthquake so severe that even today the region of the great Brahmaputra river basin hasn't settled down. Not long ago it was reported that the entire Shillong plateau had moved an appreciable distance away from the Brahmaputra towards the Bay of Bengal. According to the Geological Survey of India, this shift has been taking place gradually over the past ninety years.

Had Grandfather been alive, he would have added one more clipping to his scrapbook on the earthquake. The clipping goes in anyway, because the scrapbook is now with the children. More than newspaper accounts of the disaster, it was Grandfather's own letters and memoirs that made the earthquake seem recent and vivid; for he, along with Grandmother and two of their children (one of them my father), was living in Shillong, a picturesque little hill station in Assam*, when the earth shook and the mountains heaved.

As I have mentioned, Grandfather was in his bath, splashing about, and did not hear the first rumbling. But Grandmother was in the garden, hanging out or taking in the washing (she could never remember which) when, suddenly, the animals began making a hideous noise—a sure intimation of a natural disaster, for animals sense the approach of an earthquake much more quickly than humans.

The crows all took wing, wheeling wildly overhead and cawing loudly. The chickens flapped in circles, as if they were being chased. Two dogs sitting in the veranda suddenly jumped up and ran out with their tails between their legs. Within half a minute of her noticing the noise made by the animals, Grandmother heard a rattling, rumbling noise, like the approach of a train.

The noise increased for about a minute, and then there was the first trembling of the ground. The animals by this time seemed to have gone mad. Treetops lashed backwards and forwards, doors

*This, of course, was a long time before the state of Meghalaya, of which Shillong is now the capital, was created.

banged and windows shook, and Grandmother swore later that the house actually swayed in front of her. She had difficulty in standing straight, though this could have been due more to the trembling of her knees than to the trembling of the ground.

The first shock lasted for about a minute and a half. 'I was in my tub having a bath,' Grandfather wrote for posterity, 'which for the first time in the last two months I had taken in the afternoon instead of in the morning. My wife and children and the ayah were downstairs. Then the shock came, accompanied by a loud rumbling sound under the earth and a quaking which increased in intensity every second. It was like putting many shells in a basket and shaking them up with a rapid sifting motion from side to side.

'At first I did not realize what it was that caused my tub to sway about and the water to splash. I rose up, and found the earth heaving, while the washstand, basin, sewer, cups and glasses danced and rocked about in the most hideous fashion. I rushed to the inner door to open it and search for my wife and children, but could not move the dratted door as boxes, furniture and plaster had come up against it. The back door was the only way of escape. I managed to burst it open, and thank God, was able to get out. Sections of the thatched roof had slithered down on the four sides like a pack of cards and blocked all the exits and entrances.

'With only a towel wrapped around my waist, I ran out into the open to the front of the house, but found only my wife there. The whole front of the house was blocked by the fallen section of thatch from the roof. Through this I broke my way under the iron railings and extricated the others. The bearer had pluckily borne the weight of the whole thatched-roof section on his back as it had slithered down, and in this way saved the ayah and the children from being crushed beneath it.'

After the main shock of the earthquake had passed, minor shocks took place at regular intervals of five minutes or so, all through the night. But during that first shake-up the town of Shillong was reduced to ruin and rubble. Everything made of masonry was brought to the ground. Government House, the post office, the jail, all tumbled down. When the jail fell, the prisoners, instead of making their escape, sat huddled on the road waiting for the superintendent to come to their aid.

'The ground began to heave and shake,' wrote a young girl in a newspaper called *The Englishman**. 'I stayed on my bicycle for a second, and then fell off and got up and tried to run, staggering about from side to side of the road. To my left I saw great clouds of dust, which I afterwards discovered to be houses falling and the earth slipping from the sides

---

*This later became *The Statesman*.

of the hills. To my right I saw the small dam at the end of the lake torn asunder and the water rushing out, the wooden bridge across the lake break in two and the sides of the lake falling in; and at my feet the ground cracking and opening. I was wild with fear and didn't know which way to turn.'

The lake rose up like a mountain, and then totally disappeared, leaving only a swamp of red mud. Not a house was left standing. People were rushing about, wives looking for husbands, parents looking for children, not knowing whether their loved ones were alive or dead. A crowd of people had collected on the cricket ground, which was considered the safest place; but Grandfather and the family took shelter in a small shop on the road outside his house. The shop was a rickety wooden structure, which had always looked as though it would fall down in a strong wind. But it withstood the earthquake.

And then the rain came and it poured. This was extraordinary, because before the earthquake there wasn't a cloud to be seen; but, five minutes after the shock, Shillong was enveloped in cloud and mist. The shock was felt for more than a hundred miles on the Assam–Bengal Railway. A train was overturned at Shamshernagar; another was derailed at Mantolla. Over a thousand people lost their lives in the Cherrapunji Hills, and in other areas, too, the death toll was heavy.

The Brahmaputra burst its banks and many cultivators were drowned in the flood. A tiger was found drowned. And in north Bhagalpur, where the earthquake had started, two elephants sat down in the bazaar and refused to get up until the following morning.

Over a hundred men who were at work in Shillong's government printing press were caught in the building when it collapsed, and though the men of a Gurkha regiment did splendid rescue work, only a few were brought out alive. One of those killed in Shillong was Mr McCabe, a British official. Grandfather described the ruins of Mr McCabe's house: 'Here a bedpost, there a sword, a broken desk or chair, a bit of torn carpet, a well-known hat with its Indian Civil Service colours, battered books, all speaking reminiscences of the man we mourn.'

While most houses collapsed where they stood, Government House, it seems, 'fell backwards'. The church was a mass of red stones in ugly disorder. The organ was a tortured wreck.

A few days later the family, with other refugees, made their way to Calcutta to stay with friends or relatives. It was a slow, tedious journey, with many interruptions, for the roads and railway lines had been badly damaged and passengers had often to be transported in trolleys. Grandfather was rather struck at the stoicism displayed by an assistant engineer. At one station a telegram was handed to the engineer informing him that his bungalow had been destroyed. 'Beastly nuisance,' he observed with an aggrieved air. 'I've seen it cave in during a storm, but this is the first time it has played me such a trick on account of an earthquake.'

The family got to Calcutta to find the inhabitants of the capital in a panic; for they too had felt the quake and were expecting it to recur. The damage in Calcutta was slight compared to the devastation elsewhere, but nerves were on edge, and people slept in the open or in carriages. Cracks and fissures had appeared in a number of old buildings, and Grandfather was among the many who were worried at the proposal to fire a salute of sixty guns on Jubilee Day (the Diamond Jubilee of Queen Victoria); they felt the gunfire would bring down a number of shaky buildings. Obviously Grandfather did not wish to be caught in his bath a second time. However, Queen Victoria was not to be deprived of her salute. The guns were duly fired, and Calcutta remained standing.

Thunderstorm at Mussoorie

We are treated to one of those spectacular electric storms which are fairly frequent at this time of the year, late spring or early summer. The clouds grow very dark, then send bolts of lightning sizzling across the sky, lighting up the entire range of mountains. When the storm is directly overhead, there is hardly a pause in the frequency of the lightning; it is like a bright light being switched on and off with barely a second's interruption. And the hills tremble when thunder rumbles and booms in the valley.

John Lang, writing in Dickens's magazine *Household Words* in 1853, had this to say about one of our storms:

> I have seen a storm on the heights of Jura—such a storm as Lord Byron describes. I have seen lightning, and heard thunder in Australia; I have, off Tierra del Fuego, the Cape of Good Hope, and the coast of Java, kept watch in thunderstorms which have drowned in their roaring the human voice, and made everyone deaf and stupefied; but these storms are not to be compared with a thunderstorm at Mussoorie or Landour.

The Night the Roof Blew Off

Looking back at the experience, I suppose it was the sort of thing that should have happened in a James

Thurber story, like the dam that burst or the ghost who got in. But I wasn't thinking of Thurber at the time, although a few of his books were among the many I was trying to save from the icy rain and sleet pouring into my bedroom and study.

We have grown accustomed to sudden storms up here at seven thousand feet in the Himalayan foothills, and the old building in which I live has, for over a hundred years, received the brunt of wind and rain as they swept across the hills from the east. We'd lived in the building for over ten years without any untoward happening. It had even survived the shock of an earthquake without sustaining any major damage: it is difficult to tell the new cracks from the old.

It's a three-storeyed building, and I live on the top floor with my adopted family—three children and their parents. The roof consists of corrugated tin sheets, the ceiling of wooden boards. That's the traditional hill-station roof. Ours had held fast in many a storm, but the wind that night was stronger than we'd ever known it. It was cyclonic in its intensity, and it came rushing at us with a high-pitched eerie wail. The old roof groaned and protested at the unrelieved pressure. It took this battering for several hours, while the rain lashed against the window, and the lights kept coming and going.

There was no question of sleeping but we remained in bed for warmth and comfort. The fire had long since gone out, the chimney stack having collapsed, bringing down a shower of sooty rainwater.

After about four hours of buffeting, the roof could take it no more. My bedroom faces east, so my portion of the roof was the first to go.

The wind got under it and kept pushing, until, with a ripping, groaning sound, the metal sheets shifted from their moorings, some of them dropping with claps like thunder onto the road below. 'So that's it,' I thought, 'nothing worse can happen. As long as the ceiling stays on, I'm not getting out of my bed. We'll pick up the roof in the morning.'

Icy water cascading down on my face made me change my mind in a hurry. Leaping from my bed, I found that much of the ceiling had gone too. Water was pouring onto my open typewriter—the typewriter that had been my trusted companion for close to thirty years—and onto the bedside radio, bed covers, and clothes cupboard. The only object that wasn't receiving any rain was the potted philodendron, which could have done with a little watering.

Picking up my precious typewriter and abandoning the rest, I stumbled into the front sitting room (cum library), only to find that a similar situation had developed there. Water was pouring through the wooden slats, raining down on the bookshelves. By now I had been joined by the children, who had come to rescue me. Their section of the roof hadn't gone as yet. Their parents were struggling to close a window which had burst open, letting in lashings of wind and rain.

'Save the books!' shouted Dolly, the youngest, and that became our rallying cry for the next hour or two. I have open shelves, vulnerable to borrowers as well as the floods. Dolly and her brothers picked up armfuls of books and carried them into their room. But the floor was now awash all over the apartment, so the books had to be piled on the beds. Dolly was helping me gather up some of my manuscripts when a large field rat leapt onto the desk in front of her. Dolly squealed and ran for the door.

'It's all right,' said Mukesh, whose love of animals extends even to field rats. 'He's only sheltering himself from the storm.'

His big brother, Rakesh, whistled for our mongrel, Toby, but Toby wasn't interested in rats just then. He had taken shelter in the kitchen, the only dry spot in the house.

Two rooms were now practically roofless, and the sky was frequently lighted up for us by flashes of lightning. There were fireworks inside too, as water spluttered and crackled along a damaged electric wire. Presently, the lights went out altogether, which in some ways made the house a safer place. Prem, the children's father, is at his best in an emergency, and he had already located and lit two kerosene lamps; so we continued to transfer books, papers and clothes to the children's room.

We noticed that the water on the floor was beginning to subside a little. 'Where is it going?' asked Dolly, for we could see no outlet.

'Through the floor,' said Mukesh. 'Down to the rooms below.'

He was right. Cries of consternation from our neighbours told us that they were now having their share of the flood.

Our feet were freezing because there hadn't been time to put on enough protective footwear, and in any case, shoes and slippers were now awash. Tables and chairs were also piled high with books. I hadn't realized the considerable size of my library until that night! The available beds were pushed into the driest corner of the children's room and there, huddled in blankets and quilts, we spent the remaining hours of the night while the storm continued to threaten further mayhem.

But then the wind fell, and it began to snow. Through the door to the sitting room I could see snowflakes drifting through the gaps in the ceiling, settling on picture frames, statuettes and miscellaneous ornaments. Mundane things like a glue bottle and a plastic doll took on a certain beauty when covered with soft snow. The clock on the wall had stopped and with its covering of snow reminded me of a painting by Salvador Dali. And my shaving brush looked ready for use!

Most of us dozed off. I sensed that the direction of the wind had changed, and that it was now blowing from the west; it was making a rushing sound in the trees rather than in what remained of our roof. The clouds were scurrying away.

When dawn broke, we found the window panes encrusted with snow and icicles. Then the rising sun struck through the gaps in the ceiling and turned everything to gold. Snow crystals glinted like diamonds on the empty bookshelves. I crept into my abandoned bedroom to find the philodendron looking like a Christmas tree.

Prem went out to find a carpenter and a tinsmith, while the rest of us started putting things in the sun to dry out. And by evening, we'd got much of the roof on again. Vacant houses are impossible to find in Mussoorie, so there was no question of moving.

But it's a much-improved roof now, and I look forward to the approaching winter with some confidence!

Flames in the Forest

As Romi was about to mount his bicycle, he saw smoke rising from behind the distant line of trees.

'It looks like a forest fire,' said Prem, his friend and classmate.

'It's well to the east,' said Romi. 'Nowhere near the road.'

'There's a strong wind,' said Prem, looking at the dry leaves swirling across the road.

It was the middle of May, and it hadn't rained for several weeks. The grass was brown, the leaves of the trees covered with dust. Even though it was getting on to six o'clock in the evening, the boys' shirts were damp with sweat.

'It will be getting dark soon,' said Prem. 'You'd better spend the night at my house.'

'No, I said I'd be home tonight. My father isn't keeping well. The doctor has given me some pills for him.'

'You'd better hurry, then. That fire seems to be spreading.'

'Oh, it's far off. It will take me only forty minutes to ride through the forest. Bye, Prem—see you tomorrow!'

Romi mounted his bicycle and pedalled off down the main road of the village, scattering stray hens, stray dogs and stray villagers.

'Hey, look where you're going!' shouted an angry villager, leaping out of the way of the oncoming bicycle. 'Do you think you own the road?'

'Of course I own it,' called Romi cheerfully, and cycled on.

His own village lay about seven miles distant, on the other side of the forest; but there was only a primary school in his village, and Romi was now in high school. His father, who was a fairly wealthy sugarcane farmer, had only recently bought him the bicycle. Romi didn't care too much for school and felt there weren't enough holidays but he enjoyed the long rides and he got on well with his classmates.

He might have stayed the night with Prem had it not been for the pills which the vaid—the village doctor—had given him for his father.

Romi's father was having a backache, and the pills had been specially prepared from local herbs.

Having been given such a fine bicycle, Romi felt that the least he could do in return was to get those pills to his father as early as possible.

He put his head down and rode swiftly out of the village. Ahead of him, the smoke rose from the burning forest and the sky glowed red.

He soon left the village far behind. There was a slight climb, and Romi had to push harder on the pedals to get over the rise. Once over the top, the road went winding down to the edge of the forest.

This was the part Romi enjoyed the most. He relaxed, stopped pedalling, and allowed the bicycle to glide gently down the slope. Soon the wind was rushing past him, blowing his hair about his face and making his shirt billow out behind him. He burst into a song.

A dog from the village ran beside him, barking furiously. Romi shouted to the dog, encouraging him in the race.

Then the road straightened out, and Romi began pedalling again.

The dog, seeing the forest ahead, turned back to the village. It was afraid of the forest.

The smoke was thicker now, and Romi caught the smell of burning timber. But ahead of him the road was clear. He rode on.

It was a rough, dusty road, cut straight through the forest. Tall trees grew on either side, cutting off the last of the daylight. But the spreading glow of the fire on the right lit up the road, and giant tree-shadows danced before the boy on the bicycle.

Usually the road was deserted. This evening it was alive with wild creatures fleeing from the forest fire.

The first animal that Romi saw was a hare, leaping across the road in front of him. It was followed by several more hares. Then a band of monkeys streamed across, chattering excitedly.

They'll be safe on the other side, thought Romi. The fire won't cross the road.

But it was coming closer. And realizing this, Romi pedalled harder. In half an hour he should be out of the forest.

Suddenly, from the side of the road, several pheasants rose in the air, and with a whoosh, flew low across the path, just in front of the oncoming bicycle. Taken by surprise, Romi fell off. When he picked himself up and began brushing his clothes, he saw that his knee was bleeding. It wasn't a deep cut, but he allowed it to bleed a little, took out his handkerchief and bandaged his knee. Then he mounted the bicycle again.

He rode a bit slower now, because birds and animals kept coming out of the bushes.

Not only pheasants but smaller birds too were streaming across the road—parrots, jungle crows, owls, magpies—and the air was filled with their cries.

Everyone's on the move, thought Romi. It must be a really big fire.

He could see the flames now, reaching out from behind the trees on his right, and he could hear the crackling as the dry leaves caught fire. The air was hot on his face. Leaves, still alight or turning to cinders, floated past.

A herd of deer crossed the road and Romi had to stop until they had passed. Then he mounted again and rode on; but now, for the first time, he was feeling afraid.

From ahead came a faint clanging sound. It wasn't an animal sound, Romi was sure of that. A fire engine? There were no fire engines within fifty miles.

The clanging came nearer and Romi discovered that the noise came from a small boy who was running along the forest path, two milk cans clattering at his side.

'Teju!' called Romi, recognizing a boy from a neighbouring village. 'What are you doing out here?'

'Trying to get home, of course,' said Teju, panting along beside the bicycle.

'Jump on,' said Romi, stopping for him.

Teju was only eight or nine—a couple of years younger than Romi. He had come to deliver milk to some roadworkers, but the workers had left at the first signs of the fire, and Teju was hurrying home with his cans still full of milk.

He got up on the crossbar of the bicycle, and Romi moved on again. He was quite used to carrying friends on the crossbar.

'Keep beating your milk cans,' said Romi. 'Like that, the animals will know we are coming. My bell doesn't make enough noise. I'm going to get a horn for my cycle!'

'I never knew there were so many animals in the jungle,' said Teju. 'I saw a python in the middle of the road. It stretched right across!'

'What did you do?'

'Just kept running and jumped right over it!'

Teju continued to chatter but Romi's thoughts were on the fire, which was much closer now. Flames shot up from the dry grass and ran up the trunks of trees and along the branches. Smoke billowed out above the forest.

Romi's eyes were smarting and his hair and eyebrows felt scorched. He was feeling tired but he couldn't stop now, he had to get beyond the range of the fire. Another ten or fifteen minutes of steady riding would get them to the small wooden bridge that spanned the little river separating the forest from the sugarcane fields.

Once across the river, they would be safe. The fire could not touch them on the other side because the forest ended at the river's edge. But could they get to the river in time?

Clang, clang, clang, went Teju's milk cans. But the sounds of the fire grew louder too.

A tall silk-cotton tree, its branches leaning across the road, had caught fire. They were almost beneath it when there was a crash and a burning branch fell to the ground a few yards in front of them.

The boys had to get off the bicycle and leave the road, forcing their way through a tangle of thorny bushes on the left, dragging and pushing at the bicycle and only returning to the road some distance ahead of the burning tree.

'We won't get out in time,' said Teju, back on the crossbar, feeling disheartened.

'Yes, we will,' said Romi, pedalling with all his might. 'The fire hasn't crossed the road as yet.'

Even as he spoke, he saw a small flame leap up from the grass on the left. It wouldn't be long before more sparks and burning leaves were blown across the road to kindle the grass on the other side.

'Oh, look!' exclaimed Romi, bringing the bicycle to a sudden stop.

'What's wrong now?' asked Teju, rubbing his sore eyes. And then, through the smoke, he saw what was stopping them.

An elephant was standing in the middle of the road.

Teju slipped off the crossbar, his cans rolling on the ground, bursting open and spilling their contents.

The elephant was about forty feet away. It moved about restlessly, its big ears flapping as it turned its head from side to side, wondering which way to go.

From far to the left, where the forest was still untouched, a herd of elephants moved towards the river. The leader of the herd raised his trunk and trumpeted a call. Hearing it, the elephant on the road raised its own trunk and trumpeted a reply. Then it shambled off into the forest, in the direction of the herd, leaving the way clear.

'Come, Teju, jump on!' urged Romi. 'We can't stay here much longer!'

Teju forgot about his milk cans and pulled himself up on the crossbar. Romi ran forward with the bicycle, to gain speed, and mounted swiftly. He kept as far as possible to the left of the road, trying to ignore the flames, the crackling, the smoke, and the scorching heat.

It seemed that all the animals who could get away had done so. The exodus across the road had stopped.

'We won't stop again,' said Romi, gritting his teeth. 'Not even for an elephant!'

'We're nearly there!' said Teju. He was perking up again.

A jackal, overcome by the heat and smoke, lay in the middle of the path, either dead or unconscious. Romi did not stop. He swerved round the animal. Then he put all his strength into one final effort.

He covered the last hundred yards at top speed, and then they were out of the forest, freewheeling down the sloping road to the river.

'Look!' shouted Teju. 'The bridge is on fire!'

Burning embers had floated down on to the small wooden bridge and the dry, ancient timber had quickly caught fire. It was now burning fiercely.

Romi did not hesitate. He left the road, riding the bicycle over sand and pebbles. Then with a rush they went down the river bank and into the water.

The next thing they knew they were splashing around, trying to find each other in the darkness. 'Help!' cried Teju. 'I'm drowning!'

'Don't be silly,' said Romi. 'The water isn't deep—it's only up to the knees. Come here and grab hold of me.'

Teju splashed across and grabbed Romi by the belt.

'The water's so cold,' he said, his teeth chattering.

'Do you want to go back and warm yourself?' asked Romi. 'Some people are never satisfied. Come on, help me get the bicycle up. It's down here, just where we are standing.'

Together they managed to heave the bicycle out of the water and stand it upright.

'Now sit on it,' said Romi. 'I'll push you across.'

'We'll be swept away,' said Teju.

'No, we won't. There's not much water in the river at this time of the year. But the current is quite strong in the middle, so sit still. All right?'

'All right,' said Teju nervously.

Romi began guiding the bicycle across the river, one hand on the seat and one hand on the handlebar. The river was shallow and sluggish in midsummer; even so it was quite swift in the middle. But having got safely out of the burning forest, Romi was in no mood to let a little river defeat him.

He kicked off his shoes, knowing they would be lost, and then gripping the smooth stones of the river bed with his toes, he concentrated on keeping his balance and getting the bicycle and Teju through the middle of the stream. The water here came up to his waist, and the current would have been too strong for Teju to cross by himself. But when they reached the shallows, Teju got down and helped Romi push the bicycle.

They reached the opposite bank and sank down on the grass.

'We can rest now,' said Romi. 'But not all night—I've got some medicine to give to my father.'

He felt in his pockets and found that the pills, in their envelope, had turned to a soggy mess. 'Oh well, he has to take them with water anyway,' he said.

They watched the fire as it continued to spread through the forest. It had crossed the road down which they had come. The sky was a bright red, and the river reflected the colour of the sky.

Several elephants had found their way down to the river. They were cooling off by spraying water on each other with their trunks. Further downstream there were deer and other animals.

Romi and Teju looked at each other in the glow from the fire. They hadn't known each other very well before. But now they felt they had been friends for years.

XI
Green Notes

Poets have gone into rapture over the joys of nature, but it was the playwright and social critic George Bernard Shaw who went to the heart of the matter when he wrote: 'Except during the nine months before he draws his first breath, no man manages his affairs as well as a tree does.'

The tree sums up nature's perfection which can be seen in every leaf, flower, seed, and creatures great and small. We do not stop learning from the natural world. The earth, the seas, the heavens have still so much to tell us. Nature's notebook is never closed.

Night

New moon in a deep purple sky.

Rainy Day in June

A thunderstorm, followed by strong winds, brought down the temperature. That was yesterday. And today it is cloudy, cool, drizzling a little, almost monsoon weather; but it is still too early for the real monsoon.

The birds are enjoying the cool weather. The green-backed tits cool their bottoms in the rainwater pool. A king-crow flashes past, winging through the air like an arrow. On the wing, it snaps up a hovering dragonfly. The mynas fetch crow feathers to line their nests in the eaves of the house. I am lying so still on the window seat that a tit alights on the sill, within a few inches of my head. It snaps up a small dead moth before flying away.

At dusk I sit at the window and watch the trees

and listen to the wind as it makes light conversation in the leafy tops of the maples. There is a whirr of wings as the king-crows fly into the trees to roost for the night. But for one large bat it is time to get busy, and he flits in and out of the trees. The sky is just light enough to enable me to see the bat and the outlines of the taller trees.

Up on Landour hill, the lights are just beginning to come on. It is deliciously cool, eight o'clock, a perfect summer's evening. Prem is singing to himself in the kitchen. His wife and sister are chattering beneath the walnut tree. Down the hill, a kakar is barking, alarmed perhaps by the presence of a leopard.

The wind grows stronger and the tall maples bow before it: the maple moves its slender branches slowly from side to side, the oak moves its branches up and down. It is darker now; more lights on Landour. The cry of the barking deer has grown fainter, more distant, and now I hear a cricket singing in the bushes. The stars are out, the wind grows chilly, it is time to close the window.

Simple Pleasures

I did not feel like work this morning. And as it was raining there was nowhere to go. I tried reading a detective story, but it was one of those locked-room mysteries which usually try my patience. Gazing down at the road below didn't help because the rain had kept most people indoors. One of the simple pleasures of life is watering my plants, but Gautam had forestalled me; in fact, he'd drowned the geraniums. Another is browsing among old books, but I'd done that yesterday. So I sat down and made a list of 'simple pleasures', and came up with the following:

Listening to the cooing of doves and pigeons. But there are none in the vicinity. I remember an old well on the outskirts of Delhi; pigeons lived in the cool recesses of its walls. I wonder what happened to that well. The area is now a residential colony of multistoreyed flats.

Watching blue jays (rollers) in flight, indulging in their aerial acrobatics. Another pleasure from the plains . . .

I must get nearer home.

All right. Watching the sun come up from my bed near the window. But this morning there wasn't any sun!

Walking barefoot over dew-drenched grass: if only the rain would stop!

Peeling an orange. Except that they're out of season.

Then the rain stopped, the sun came out, and so did a swarm of yellow butterflies in compensation for the morning's absence of simple pleasures.

The Old Conservationists

That the Doon valley is well forested today is due mainly to the early efforts of the forest department. Up to 1864 a free system of felling was prevalent, and we find Mr O'Callaghan, Deputy Conservator of Forests, writing in 1879:

> There can be no doubt that sal, tun and shisham were the trees chiefly felled, for even now there is no demand for any other kind of timber; and when I entered the department in 1854 the ground was everywhere studded with stumps of those trees.

Restrictions were gradually imposed, but no real conservation was attempted until the 1880s. By then, all that was valuable had already been cut, and the main duty of the department was to encourage replanting and foster new generations of trees, those very trees which conservationists are striving to protect today.

Those who look with horror upon the denudation of our hills might well look back on the situation that confronted a settlement officer over a hundred years ago. In the Jaunsar area, all misfortunes were believed to be due to the machinations of one or the other of their demon spirits; and in the *Gazetteer* of that period we read that the 'people of Chijal, being afflicted with smallpox, burnt down four hundred deodar trees as a sacrifice'.

Where Have All the Trees Gone?

The peace and quiet of the Maplewood hillside disappeared forever one winter. The powers-that-be decided to build another new road into the mountains, and the PWD saw fit to take it right past the cottage, about six feet from the large window which had overlooked the forest.

In my journal I wrote: already they have felled most of the trees. The walnut was one of the first to go, a tree I had lived with for over ten years, watching it grow just as I had watched Prem's little son, Rakesh, grow up . . . Looking forward to its new leaf-buds, the broad, green leaves of summer, turning to spears of gold in September when the walnuts were ripe and ready to fall. I knew this tree better than the others. It was just below the window, where a buttress for the road is going up.

Another tree I'll miss is the young deodar, the only one growing in this stretch of the woods. Some years back it was stunted from lack of sunlight. The oaks covered it with their shaggy branches. So I cut away some of the overhanging branches and after that the deodar grew much faster. It was just coming into its own this year, now cut down in its prime like my younger brother on the road to Delhi last month: both victims of the roads. The tree killed by the PWD: my brother by a truck.

Twenty oaks have been felled just in this small stretch near the cottage. By the time this bypass reaches Jabarkhet, about six miles from here, over a thousand oaks will have been slaughtered, besides many other fine trees—maples, deodars and pines—most of them unnecessarily, as they grew some fifty to sixty yards from the roadside.

The trouble is, hardly anyone (with the exception of the contractor who buys the felled trees) really believes that trees and shrubs are necessary. They get in the way so much, don't they? According to my milkman, the only useful tree is one which can be picked clean of its leaves for fodder! And a young man remarked to me: 'You should come to Pauri. The view is terrific, there are no trees in the way!'

Well, he can stay here now, and enjoy the view of the ravaged hillside. But as the oaks have gone, the milkman will have to look further afield for his fodder.

Rakesh calls the maples the butterfly trees because, when the winged seeds fall, they flutter like butterflies in the breeze. No maples now. No bright red leaves to flame against the sky. No birds!

That is to say, no birds near the house. No longer will it be possible for me to open the window and watch the scarlet minivets flitting through the dark green foliage of the oaks; the long-tailed magpies gliding through the trees; the barbet calling insistently from his perch on top of the deodar. Forest birds, all of them, will now be in search of some other stretch of surviving forest. The only visitors will be the crows, who have learnt to live with, and off, humans, and seem to multiply along with roads, houses and people. And even when all the people have gone, the crows will still be around.

Other things to look forward to: trucks thundering past in the night, perhaps a tea and pakora shop around the corner, the grinding of gears, the music of motor horns. Will the whistling-thrush be heard above them? The explosions that continually shatter the silence of the mountains, as thousand-year-old rocks are dynamited, have frightened away all but the most intrepid of birds and animals. Even the bold langurs haven't shown their faces for over a fortnight.

Somehow, I don't think we shall wait for the tea shop to arrive. There must be some other quiet corner, possibly on the next mountain, where new roads have yet to come into being. No doubt this is a negative attitude, and if I had any sense I'd open my own tea shop. To retreat is to be a loser. But the trees are losers too; and when they fall, they do so with a certain dignity.

Never mind. Men come and go; the mountains remain.

Perfection

The smallest insect in the world is a sort of firefly and its body is only a fifth of a millimetre long. One can only just see it with the naked eye. Almost like a speck of dust, yet it has perfect little wings and little combs on its legs for preening itself.

That is perfection.

A Bedbug Gives Thanks

I'm a child of the Universe
Claimed the bug
As he crawled out of the woodwork.
I've every right
To be a blight.
To Infinite Intelligence I owe
My place—

Chief pest
Upon the human race!
I'm here to stay—
To feast upon their delicate display,
Those luscious thighs,
Those nooks and crannies
Where the blood runs sweet.
No, no, I don't despise
These creatures made for my delight.
A kind Creator had my needs in mind . . .
I thank you, Lord, for human-kind . . .

The Snake

When, after days of rain,
The sun appears,
The snake emerges
Green-gold on the grass.
Kept in so long,
He basks for hours,
Soaks up the hot bright sun.
Knowing how shy he is of me,
I walk a gentle pace,
Letting him doze in peace.
But to the snake, earth bound,
Each step must sound like thunder.

He glides away,
Goes underground.
I've known him for some years:
A harmless green grass snake
Who, when he sees me on the path,
Uncoils and disappears.

The Miracle of the Cosmos

A good year for the cosmos flower. Banks of them everywhere. They like the day-long sun; clean and fresh, this month's flower, en masse. But by itself, the wild commelina, sky blue against dark green, always catches at the heart.

My Way

Holi brings warmer days, ladybirds, new friends. Trees in new leaf. The fresh light green of the maples is very soothing.

I may not have contributed anything towards the progress of civilization, but neither have I robbed the world of anything. Not one tree or bush or bird or flower. Even the spider on my wall is welcome to his (her) space.

But I must confess to having swatted the odd mosquito. And if you have read my Introduction you will understand why I am a little wary of bees and wasps.

Brief Memories

No one lived on the hill, except occasionally a coal burner in a temporary grass-thatched hut. But villagers used the path, grazing their sheep and cattle on the grassy slopes. Each cow or sheep had a bell suspended from its neck, to let the shepherd boy know of its whereabouts. The boy could then lie in the sun and eat wild strawberries without fear of losing his animals.

I remembered some of the shepherd boys and girls.

There was a boy who played a flute. Its rough, sweet, straightforward notes travelled clearly across the mountain air. He would greet me with a nod of his head, without taking the flute off from his lips. There was a girl who was nearly always cutting grass for fodder. She wore heavy bangles on her feet, and long silver earrings. She did not speak much either, but she always had a wide grin on her face when she met me on the path. She used to sing to herself, or to the sheep, to the grass, or to the sickle in her hand.

And there was a boy who carried milk into town (a distance of about five miles), who would often fall into step with me, to hold a long conversation. He had never been away from the hills, or in a large city. He had never been in a train. I told him about the cities, and he told me about his village; how they make bread from maize, how fish were to be caught in the mountain streams, how the bears came to steal his father's pumpkins. Whenever the pumpkins were ripe, he told me, the bears would come and carry them off.

These things I remembered—these, and the smell of pine needles, the silver of oak leaves and the red of maple, the call of the Himalayan cuckoo, and the mist, like a wet face cloth, pressing against the hills.

Odd, how some little incident, some snatch of conversation, comes back to one again and again, in the most unlikely places. Standing in the aisle of a crowded tube train on a Monday morning, years ago, in another country, my nose tucked into the back page of someone else's newspaper, I suddenly had a vision of a bear making off with a ripe pumpkin.

A bear and a pumpkin—and there, between Goodge Street and Tottenham Court Road stations, all the smells and sounds of the Himalayas came rushing back to me.

Survivors

I may not love weeds (in the same sense that I love flowers), but I do respect and admire them, basically, for their ability to flourish in the most unlikely and even hostile places, putting up with exhaust fumes, trampling feet, traffic, bulldozers, roadside tenements, grazing cattle and goats, giving one hope that not all the world's plant life will be extinct by the end of this century.

Monsoon Visitors

A cicada starts up in the tree nearest to my window seat. What has he been doing all these weeks, and why does he choose this particular moment and this particular evening to play the fiddle so loudly? The cicadas are late this year, the monsoon has been late. But soon the forest will be ringing with the sound of the cicadas—an orchestra constantly tuning up but never quite getting into tune—and the sound of the birds will be pushed into the background.

Outside the front door I found an elegant young praying mantis reclining on a leaf of the honeysuckle creeper. I say young because he hadn't grown to his full size, and was that very tender pale green which is the colour of a young mantis. They are light brown to begin with, like dry twigs, but as they grow older and the monsoon foliage becomes greener, they too change, and by mid-August they are dark green.

As though to make up for lost time, the monsoon rains are now here with a vengeance. It has been pouring all day, and already the roof is leaking. But nothing dampens Prem's spirits. He is still singing love songs in the kitchen.

After the Monsoon

Towards the end of the year, those few monsoon clouds that still linger over the Himalayas are no longer burdened with rain and are able to assume unusual shapes and patterns, chasing each other across the sky and disappearing in spectacular sunset formations.

I have always found this to be the best time of the year in the hills. The sun-drenched hillsides are still an emerald green; the air is crisp, but winter's bite is still a month or two away; and for those who still like to take to the open road on foot, there are springs, streams, and waterfalls tumbling over rocks that remain dry for most of the year. The lizard that basked on a sun-baked slab of granite last May is missing, but in his place the spotted forktail trips daintily among the boulders in a stream; and the strident sound of the cicadas is gradually replaced by the gentler trilling of the crickets and grasshoppers.

Now, more than at any other time of the year, the wild flowers come into their own.

The hillside is covered with flowers and ferns. Sprays of wild, ginger, tangles of clematis, flat clusters of yarrow and lady's mantle. The datura grows everywhere with its graceful white balls and prickly fruits. And then, of course, there is the delicate commelina, a breathtaking sight. It always stops me in my tracks. I forget the world.

But only for a moment. The blare of a truck's horn reminds me that I am still lingering on the main road leading out of the hill station. A cloud of dust and a blast of diesel fumes are further indications that reality takes many different forms, assailing all my senses at once! Even my commelina seems to shrink from the onslaught. But as long as it is still there, I take heart and leave the highway for a lesser road.

Acknowledgements

My thanks to Ravi Singh and Meru Gokhale for their help and suggestions in making this selection from my published and new writings. My thanks also to Puja Prakash for the beautiful cover design.